THE THEOLOGY OF THE FIRST LETTER TO THE CORINTHIANS

This study shows that the common view of 1 Corinthians as mainly about "ethics" and therefore of little importance for "theology" needs correcting. Furnish argues that 1 Corinthians is an even better place to take the apostle's theological pulse than the allegedly "more theological" letters to the Galatians and Romans, because here it is especially evident how this thinking about the gospel took place within the crucible of his missionary and pastoral labors. Paul's complex theological legacy is not a systematic theology or even the basis for constructing a theological system. However, we come close to the heart of Paul's legacy in his clear-sighted identification of the gospel with the saving power of God's love as disclosed in Christ, and his insistence that those who are called to belong to Christ are thereby summoned to be agents of God's love wherever in the world they have received that call.

Victor Paul Furnish is University Distinguished Professor of New Testament in Southern Methodist University's Perkins School of Theology. He has written several books, including *The Moral Teaching of Paul: Selected Issues* (second edition, 1985), *II Corinthians* (Anchor Bible 32A, 1984), and *Jesus According to Paul* (1993). In addition, Furnish has contributed to a number of other volumes, including *Pauline Theology*, vol. II (edited by D. M. Hay, 1993) and vol. IV (edited by D. M. Hay and E. E. Johnson, 1997), *Caught in the Crossfire: Helping the Church Debate Homosexuality* (edited by S. Geis and D. Messer, 1994), and *Homosexuality in the Church: Both Sides of the Debate* (edited by J. S. Siker, 1994).

NEW TESTAMENT THEOLOGY

General editor: James D. G. Dunn,
Lightfoot Professor of Divinity, University of Durham

This series sets out to provide a programmatic survey of the individual writings of the New Testament. It aims to remedy the deficiency of available published material which concentrates on the New Testament writers' theological concerns. New Testament specialists here write at greater length than is usually possible in the introduction to commentaries or as part of other New Testament theologies, and explore the theological themes and issues of their chosen books without being tied to a commentary format, or to a thematic structure provided from elsewhere. When complete, the series will cover all the New Testament writings, and will thus provide an attractive, and timely, range of texts around which courses can be developed.

Titles published in this series

THE THEOLOGY OF THE FIRST LETTER TO THE CORINTHIANS

VICTOR PAUL FURNISH

University Distinguished Professor of New Testament,
Southern Methodist University

PUBLISHED BY THE PRESS SYNDICATE OF THE UNIVERSITY OF CAMBRIDGE
The Pitt Building, Trumpington Street, Cambridge CB2 1RP, United Kingdom

CAMBRIDGE UNIVERSITY PRESS
The Edinburgh Building, Cambridge CB2 2RU, United Kingdom
http://www.cup.cam.ac.uk
40 West 20th Street, New York, NY 10011–4211, USA http://www.cup.org
10 Stamford Road, Oakleigh, Melbourne 3166, Australia

First published 1999

Printed in the United Kingdom at the University Press, Cambridge

Typeset in Baskerville MT 11/12.5pt [SE]

A catalogue record for this book is available from the British Library

Library of Congress Cataloguing in Publication data
Furnish, Victor Paul.
   The Theology of the first letter to the Corinthians/Victor Paul Furnish.
      p.   cm. – (New Testament Theology)
   Includes bibliographical references and indexes.
   ISBN 0 521 35252 5 (hardback) – ISBN 0 521 35807 8 (paperback)
   1. Bible. N. T. Corinthians, 1st Criticism, interpretation, etc.   2. Bible. N. T.
   Corinthians, 1st – Theology.   I. Title.   II. Series
   BS2675.2.F87   1989
   227'.206–dc21   98–35136 CIP

ISBN 0 521 35252 5 hardback
ISBN 0 521 35807 8 paperback

To
Schubert M. Ogden
valued colleague, cherished friend

Contents

x   *Contents*

Editor's preface

Although the New Testament is usually taught within Departments or Schools or Faculties of Theology/Divinity/Religion, theological study of the individual New Testament writings is often minimal or at best patchy. The reasons for this are not hard to discern.

For one thing, the traditional style of studying a New Testament document is by means of straight exegesis, often verse by verse. Theological concerns jostle with interesting historical, textual, grammatical and literary issues, often at the cost of the theological. Such exegesis is usually very time-consuming, so that only one or two key writings can be treated in any depth within a crowded three-year syllabus.

For another, there is a marked lack of suitable textbooks round which courses could be developed. Commentaries are likely to lose theological comment within a mass of other detail in the same way as exegetical lectures. The section on the theology of a document in the Introduction to a commentary is often very brief and may do little more than pick out elements within the writing under a sequence of headings drawn from systematic theology. Excursuses usually deal with only one or two selected topics. Likewise larger works on New Testament Theology usually treat Paul's letters as a whole and, having devoted the great bulk of the space to Jesus, Paul and John, can spare only a few pages for others.

In consequence, there is little incentive on the part of teacher or student to engage with a particular New Testament document, and students have to be content with a general overview, at best complemented by in-depth study of (parts of) two or three New Testament writings. A serious corollary to this is the degree to which students are thereby incapacitated in the task of integrating their New Testament study with the rest of their Theology or Religion courses, since often they are capable only of drawing on the general overview or on a sequence of particular verses treated atomistically. The growing importance of a literary-critical approach to individual documents simply highlights the present deficiencies even more. Having been given little experience in handling individual New Testament writings as such at a theological level, most students are very ill-prepared to develop a properly integrated literary and theological response to particular texts. Ordinands too need more help than they currently receive from textbooks, so that their preaching from particular passages may be better informed theologically.

There is need therefore for a series to bridge the gap between too brief an introduction and too full a commentary where theological discussion is lost among too many other concerns. It is our aim to provide such a series. That is, a series where New Testament specialists are able to write at a greater length on the theology of individual writings than is usually possible in the introductions to commentaries or as part of New Testament Theologies, and to explore the theological themes and issues of these writings without being tied to a commentary format or to a thematic structure provided from elsewhere. The volumes seek both to describe each document's theology, and to engage theologically with it, noting also its canonical context and any specific influence it may have had on the history of Christian faith and life. They are directed at those who already have one or two years of full-time New Testament and theological study behind them.

University of Durham   JAMES D. G. DUNN

Preface

Paul consistently refers to himself as an "apostle," as one who has been specifically commissioned to proclaim the gospel among the Gentiles, to establish churches, and to nurture believers in their faith. He nowhere refers to himself as a "theologian." Moreover, although the word "theology" is often employed in other ancient Greek religious texts, it does not once appear in his letters (or anywhere else in the New Testament or in the Greek version of the Hebrew Bible). Thus Paul's writings must be approached first of all as *apostolic letters*, not as theological documents. They are all more or less situation-specific, having been prompted by and addressed to issues that were current in particular congregations, or for Paul himself. For this reason, any examination of "the theology of 1 Corinthians" must begin with some consideration of whether it is appropriate to speak of "Pauline theology" at all, and if so, in what sense.[1]

The Greek word *theologia* (literally, "discourse about [a] god") seems to have been introduced into Christian circles only in the second century. At first it was used in rather general ways, with reference to "teaching about divine things" or, yet more generally, with reference to "religious speech." The earliest surviving reference to Paul as a "theologian" may be in the works of Athanasius, sometime bishop of Alexandria (d. 373). Introducing a quotation from the letter to the Romans, Athanasius commented that he had learned much "from the theologians, of whom one is Paul" (*Against the Pagans* 35.18–20). Here "the theologians" in view are the authors

---

[1] See also my essay, "Paul the Theologian," in *The Conversation Continues: Studies in Paul & John. In Honor of J. Louis Martyn* (ed. by Robert T. Fortna and Beverly R. Gaventa; Nashville, 1990), 19–34.

of Scripture, whom Athanasius described as such because he believed them to be divinely inspired, not because he regarded them as concerned with doctrines or systems of doctrine (*On the Incarnation* 56.6–10; cf. *Against the Pagans* 1.9–10).

The word "theology" was not used with reference to comprehensive, systematic presentations of Christian doctrine until the twelfth century, in works by scholastic thinkers like Abelard and Peter Lombard. The influence of this medieval usage is apparent whenever Paul's theology is identified with what he says about the traditional topics of systematic theology – God, creation, sin, salvation, Christ, the Spirit, the church, eschatology, and the like. Yet the fact remains that Paul himself did not construct a "theology" in the scholastic sense. All attempts to mine his letters for the components of a theological system run the double risk of imposing on his thought what is not there and of missing what is there.

Since Paul himself did not develop a theological system, and because the traditional categories of systematic theology more often obscure his thought than clarify it, why not abandon the attempt to discern anything like a Pauline "theology"? Why not attend simply to the apostle's "practical" teachings, and to what can be inferred from his letters about the appeals that characterized his missionary preaching? For instance, one recent interpreter has argued that "it is a fundamental mistake" to regard Paul "as the 'prince of thinkers' and the Christian 'theologian par excellence,'" since he was "first and foremost a missionary, a man of practical religion," whose thought defies logical analysis.[2] One should of course take care not simply to presume that Paul was always consistent, either in his thinking or in his articulation of his views. Yet his letters leave no doubt that certain firmly held religious convictions shaped and informed his preaching and teaching. Moreover, the apostle himself often identified, explicated, and even conceptualized those convictions in order to support and commend his understanding of the gospel and of Christian faith.

There is in fact a growing consensus that one need not, indeed must not, choose between Paul the "thinker" and Paul the "practical man." To understand Paul the apostle one must understand

---

[2] Heikki Räisänen, *Paul and the Law* (Philadelphia, 1986), 266–67; see also 1–15.

the way he himself reflected on his gospel, since this is what gave his ministry its special direction and shape. Precisely because he was an *apostle*, he was devoted to thinking through, and to helping others think through, the truth and significance of that gospel. Recognizing this, interpreters are increasingly concerned to find ways of approaching his thought that will do justice both to its own structure and to the situational contexts of his letters within which it finds expression. These letters certainly do not yield "a theology," if by that one means an orderly, consistent construct of beliefs about God and human existence. What they do yield is a portrait of Paul as "theologian," in that they disclose him engaged in serious reflection on Christian understandings of God and of human existence, and concerned to communicate those understandings to others intelligibly, and in a way that will make a difference in their lives.

It is therefore with Paul's *theological reflection* in 1 Corinthians that the present study is concerned. This is most evident where he is engaged in the exposition, sometimes rather extended, of particular assertions or claims. But it also comes into view when he offers interpretive comments on Scripture or statements drawn from the church's tradition, when he states his own strongly held beliefs concerning the truth and significance of the gospel, and not least, when he mounts arguments against understandings of the gospel that differ from his own.

When interpreting these passages and statements one must take care not to import ideas and themes that surface in other Pauline letters, as if the apostle's thinking always started at the same place, followed the same course, and arrived at the same conclusions. An assessment of his theological reflection in 1 Corinthians has to proceed with constant reference to the specific aims and character of this particular letter. Moreover, one must not forget what prompts Paul's theological reflection and drives his concern to elucidate the gospel. It is not an interest in establishing a specific set of beliefs to which he can then demand that the Corinthians give their assent. Rather, it is the conviction that he is obligated to deepen his hearers'[3] understanding of the gospel in order that their

---

[3] "Hearers" rather than "readers," because upon receipt the apostle's letter would have been read aloud to the congregation.

lives may be more fully conformed to it, both as a community of faith and as people called to live out their faith in the everyday world.

My understanding of the theological orientation of 1 Corinthians has been significantly enriched and informed through participation in the Pauline Theology Group, which met annually from 1986 through 1995 under the auspices of the Society of Biblical Literature. For the privilege of membership in that group and the opportunities it afforded for collegial dialogue, I am deeply grateful.[4] My gratitude extends as well to James D. G. Dunn, also a member of that group, for inviting me to contribute to his New Testament Theology series, and then for waiting so patiently while I completed my assignment; to the Perkins School of Theology, Southern Methodist University, for grants of a faculty research leave and a Scholarly Outreach Award which gave me extra time to work on this volume; to Mr. Katsuya Kawano, for preparing the indexes; and by no means least to the longtime friend and colleague to whom this book is dedicated, from whom I continue to learn so much.

Unless otherwise noted, the translations of biblical materials are my own.

[4] For the results of the Group's work, see *Pauline Theology*, I–III (edited respectively by Jouette M. Bassler; David M. Hay; and David M. Hay and E. Elizabeth Johnson; Minneapolis, 1991–95), and IV (ed. by E. Elizabeth Johnson and David M. Hay; Atlanta, 1997).

Abbreviations

AB	The Anchor Bible
AGJU	Arbeiten zur Geschichte des antiken Judentums und des Urchristentums
ANRW	*Aufstieg und Niedergang der römischen Welt*
ANTC	Abingdon New Testament Commentaries
BA	*Biblical Archaeologist*
BARev	*Biblical Archaeology Review*
BETL	Bibliotheca ephemeridum theologicarum lovaniensium
BEvT	Beiträge zur evangelischen Theologie
BGBE	Beiträge zur Geschichte der biblischen Exegese
BHT	Beiträge zur historischen Theologie
BNTC	Black's New Testament Commentaries
BWANT	Beiträge zur Wissenschaft vom Alten und Neuen Testament
CBQ	*Catholic Biblical Quarterly*
EDNT	*Exegetical Dictionary of the New Testament*
EKKNT	Evangelisch-katholischer Kommentar zum Neuen Testament
FRLANT	Forschungen zur Religion und Literatur des Alten und Neuen Testaments
GNS	Good News Studies
HNT	Handbuch zum Neuen Testament
HUT	Hermeneutische Untersuchungen zur Theologie
ICC	International Critical Commentary
Interp	*Interpretation*
JAAR	*Journal of the American Academy of Religion*
JBL	*Journal of Biblical Literature*

JSNT	*Journal for the Study of the New Testament*
JSNTSup	*Journal for the Study of the New Testament* – Supplement Series
JTS	*Journal of Theological Studies*
KD	*Kerygma und Dogma*
KEK	Kritisch-exegetischer Kommentar über das Neue Testament
MNTC	Moffatt New Testament Commentary
NIB	*The New Interpreter's Bible*
NICNT	New International Commentary on the New Testament
NIGTC	The New International Greek Testament Commentary
NovT	*Novum Testamentum*
NovTSup	*Novum Testamentum* – Supplement series
NTAbh	Neutestamentliche Abhandlungen
NTD	Das Neue Testament Deutsch
NTS	*New Testament Studies*
RB	*Revue biblique*
RevExp	*Review and Expositor*
SBLDS	Society of Biblical Literature Dissertation Series
SBLSBS	Society of Biblical Literature Sources for Biblical Study
SBS	Stuttgarter Bibelstudien
SBT	Studies in Biblical Theology
SNT	Studien zum Neuen Testament
SNTSMS	Society of New Testament Studies Monograph Series
SNTU	*Studien zum Neuen Testament und seiner Umwelt*
SUNT	Studien zur Umwelt des Neuen Testaments
TDNT	*Theological Dictionary of the New Testament*
TDOT	*Theological Dictionary of the Old Testament*
THKNT	Theologischer Handkommentar zum Neuen Testament
TS	*Theological Studies*
TU	Texte und Untersuchungen
VC	*Vigiliae christianae*
VCS	Variorum Collected Studies

WBC	Word Biblical Commentary
WD	*Wort und Dienst*
WUNT	Wissenschaftliche Untersuchungen zum Neuen Testament
ZNW	*Zeitschrift für die neutestamentliche Wissenschaft*
ZTK	*Zeitschrift für Theologie und Kirche*

CHAPTER I

Introduction

Paul's theological reflection in 1 Corinthians, as in his other letters, stands in the service of his apostolic ministry. It is therefore important to begin with a brief review of the origins and course of the apostle's Corinthian ministry, to take special note of what occasioned his writing of 1 Corinthians, and to offer some preliminary observations about the contents of this letter and certain of its formal characteristics.

PAUL AND THE CORINTHIANS

More is known about the Corinthian church, including Paul's relationships with it, than about any other first-century congregation. This is due not only to the extent but also to the character of 1 and 2 Corinthians, our primary sources of information. In these letters, more than in others, Paul is dealing with topics that are specific to the Corinthians' situation and to his own standing as their apostle. Even so, we must remember that Paul himself may not have been well informed about some aspects of the Corinthian situation, that in any case we are privy only to his point of view, and that any historical reconstruction like the one attempted here necessarily remains both incomplete and hypothetical.

The apostle's first visit

Ancient Corinth was strategically located somewhat south and west of the narrow isthmus of land that connects the northern part of Greece with the Peloponnesus. The city was served by two ports, Cenchreae on the Saronic Gulf to the southeast and Lechaeum on the Gulf of Corinth to the northwest. Ships were regularly unloaded in one port and their cargoes transported across the isthmus for reloading at the other port, thus providing a link between shipping in the Aegean and the Adriatic. By reason of its proximity to this vital link between east and west, and because it also commanded the overland routes running north and south, Corinth was an important commercial center.

The old Greek city of Corinth had been virtually destroyed by the Romans in 146 BCE, but in 44 BCE Julius Caesar provided for the resettlement of the site as a Roman colony. By Paul's day Corinth was once more a flourishing urban center, its population likely numbering in the tens of thousands. This was an ethnically, culturally, and religiously very diverse population, in part because the original colonists had been mainly freed slaves recruited from the ranks of Rome's poor. Thus many of them would have been Syrians, Egyptians, and Jews. There were, in addition, Greeks native to the area, and then in subsequent years people from all parts of the Mediterranean world, attracted to the city in hope of increasing their fortune and their status.

Corinth was not only important as a center of trade and commerce, but in Paul's day it served also as the capital of the Roman province of Achaia. It was therefore the place of residence of the Roman proconsul, appointed annually. Moreover, the Corinth that Paul knew had regained its role as administrator of the famed Isthmian Games, held every two years at a site on the isthmus just a few miles from the center of the city. These athletic and cultural events, dedicated to the sea-god, Poseidon (known to the Romans as Neptune), added to the already large numbers of visitors coming to Corinth by reason of its commercial and political importance.

Some commentaries on the Corinthian letters continue to describe Roman Corinth as a center of unspeakable sexual debauchery. There is no evidence, however, that this was the case. Indeed, what most controlled the city's life and defined its moral character was not sexual decadence, but a relentless competition for social status, honor, wealth, and power. In this respect it was not unlike other urban centers of the day, where people with means could hope to gain higher social standing and greater honor by contributing to the public welfare, and by becoming the patrons of those who needed their support and would lionize them for it. It was to such a city that Paul came preaching the gospel of Christ.[1]

The earliest surviving letter written by Paul, 1 Thessalonians, was very likely dispatched sometime during his first period of residency in Corinth. From this letter one learns something about the apostle's itinerary, beginning with his mission to the Macedonian city of Philippi. He tells the Thessalonians that even though his missionary team "had . . . suffered and been terribly mistreated" in Philippi, they had gone on to Thessalonica still preaching the gospel (1 Thess. 2.1–2). After some time in that city (during which the Philippians sent them aid "more than once," Phil. 4.16), Paul and his associates proceeded to Athens, in Achaia; but, perhaps fairly soon, Timothy was sent back to Thessalonica in order to check on the situation there (1 Thess. 3.1–5).

First Thessalonians was written after Timothy's return from Macedonia (3.6), and when Silvanus, too, was with Paul (1.1). The apostle refers to Athens as if he is no longer there (3.1), so he and his two companions are probably now in Corinth. This would correspond with 2 Corinthians 1.19, where Paul names both Silvanus and Timothy as having participated in the mission to Corinth. It also agrees with the itinerary presented in Acts, where Paul's European mission proceeds from Philippi (16.11–40) to Thessalonica (17.1–9), then subsequently to Beroea (17.10–14), to Athens (17.15–34), and finally to Corinth (18.1). In Corinth the apostle is joined by Silas (Silvanus) and Timothy (18.5).

What was the gospel that Paul, Silvanus, and Timothy brought to Corinth? What were the themes of their missionary preaching in this sprawling urban center? When the apostle himself ventures to characterize the gospel that he had proclaimed there, he does so with reference to Jesus. Jesus had been presented to the Corinthians as the "crucified" one (1 Cor. 2.2), as "the Son of God" (2 Cor. 1.19), and as "Lord" (2 Cor. 4.5). It corresponds to this that

---

[1] More detailed comments about Roman Corinth are offered by Jerome Murphy-O'Connor, *St. Paul's Corinth: Texts and Archaeology*, GNS 6 (Collegeville, MN, [1990? © 1983]), and V. P. Furnish, *II Corinthians*, AB 32A (Garden City, NY, 1984), 4–22. See also: John K. Chow, *Patronage and Power: A Study of Social Networks in Corinth*, JSNTSup 75 (Sheffield, 1992); and Andrew D. Clarke, *Secular and Christian Leadership in Corinth: A Socio-Historical and Exegetical Study of 1 Corinthians 1–6*, AGJU 18 (Leiden, New York, and Cologne, 1993).

Paul can accuse others of having preached "another Jesus" in Corinth (2 Cor. 11.4). He also refers to certain traditions that he had handed on to the Corinthians, especially those about the saving significance of Jesus' death (1 Cor. 15.3; see also 11.23–26; 8.11) and Jesus' resurrection and resurrection appearances (1 Cor. 15.4–8, 12, 15). Further, what can be inferred from 1 Thessalonians 1.9–10 about Paul's missionary preaching in Thessalonica perhaps holds good for his message in Corinth as well (especially if 1 Thessalonians was written during Paul's initial visit to Corinth): there is one true and living God; Jesus is God's Son, resurrected from the dead; and Jesus will return to bring salvation from the coming wrath.

Paul must have remained in Corinth for a substantial period of time. The eighteen months mentioned in Acts 18.11 is not unreasonable, since 1 Corinthians attests that the congregation was relatively large and well established by the end of his first visit (see also Acts 18.10). In addition, he was there long enough to have experienced difficulties in supporting himself. Even though constantly plying his trade as a tentmaker (Acts 18.3), he was forced to depend to some extent on help from congregations that he had founded earlier (2 Cor. 11.9). Paul's departure from Corinth seems to have been hastened by serious opposition, perhaps emanating from the city's Jewish community (Acts 18.6–11). This had apparently culminated in some kind of a hearing before the Roman proconsul, Gallio (Acts 18.12–17). If Gallio's term of office began in July of 51, as seems likely, and if in fact Paul had been in Corinth for something like eighteen months, then this first visit probably began in late 49 or early 50, and continued on into the summer of 51.[2]

The converts

The apostle's extended residency in Corinth allowed him the opportunity not only to preach the gospel but also to organize his converts into a congregation. His preaching must have included a call to undergo baptism into Christ, and thus into the Christian community (see, e.g., 1 Cor. 12.13), even though he downplays the

---

[2] For this dating see, especially, Murphy-O'Connor, *St. Paul's Corinth*, 137–60.

number of persons whom he himself had baptized (1 Cor. 1.14–17). Most of all, Paul keeps reminding the Corinthians that *his* gospel is the one to which they were converted: he is their parent in the faith (1 Cor. 3.1–2; 4.15; 2 Cor. 12.14–15), the one who "planted" the gospel among them (1 Cor. 3.6), the one who laid the "foundation" for their faith by proclaiming Jesus Christ (1 Cor. 3.10–11). He thus distinguishes himself from other preachers, most especially from Apollos, a Jewish Christian of Alexandrian origin who came to Corinth only later to "water" the congregation that Paul had already planted (1 Cor. 3.6; cf. Acts 18.24–19.1).

A number of the people who were converted during the apostle's first visit to Corinth are known to us by name. Stephanas and his household are identified as the very first to accept the gospel and are warmly commended for their service to the church (1 Cor. 16.15–16). They were among those Paul acknowledges having baptized (1 Cor. 1.16), as were Gaius and Crispus (1 Cor. 1.14). Gaius is also mentioned in Romans 16.23 as the host of a house church. Both he and Stephanas were Gentile converts, while Crispus, assuming he is the same one named in Acts 18.8, was Jewish – indeed, the former head of the local synagogue.[3] Two other Gentile converts were Fortunatus and Achaicus. Along with Stephanas, they happen to be with Paul as he writes 1 Corinthians (1 Cor. 16.17–18). The apostle also mentions "Chloe's people" as having come from Corinth (1 Cor. 1.11), which was more likely their home base than Ephesus. They were probably slaves, or at least in the employ of Chloe, who must have been a woman of some standing in the city. However, there is no way to determine whether she too was a member of the Corinthian congregation.

According to Acts, Paul's first hosts in Corinth were a Jewish-Christian couple, Aquila and Priscilla (Prisca), who themselves had recently arrived in the city from Rome (Acts 18.1–4). It is unclear whether they were already Christians when they came to Corinth or were converted only after meeting Paul there. The apostle apparently became acquainted with them in the process of establishing

---

[3] Another synagogue official, Sosthenes, is mentioned in Acts 18.17. He was perhaps Gaius' successor. If perchance he is the same Sosthenes who joins Paul in sending 1 Corinthians (1 Cor. 1.1), then he too can be listed as one of the apostle's early converts in the city; but the identification is by no means certain.

himself as a tradesman in Corinth, for they too were tentmakers. However, their subsequent partnership with Paul in the service of the gospel (Rom. 16.3), along with their hosting a house church (Rom. 16.5; 1 Cor. 16.19), became much more important for him than their partnership with him in business. In addition, some-where along the line – under what circumstances we do not know – they put their own safety at risk in order to save the apostle's life (Rom. 16.4).

Another of Paul's early converts in Corinth was a certain Titius Justus. The author of Acts describes him as having been "a wor-shiper of God" (18.7, NRSV), meaning that he was a Gentile who had associated himself with the monotheistic beliefs of the Jews, but without having become a Jew himself. Persons of this sort, in Corinth and elsewhere, were especially good prospects for conver-sion to Christianity.

The roster of early Corinthian converts could perhaps be extended to include at least some of those from whom Paul conveys greetings in Romans 16, a chapter that was almost certainly written in Corinth during the apostle's third visit to his congregation. But except for Gaius (Rom. 16.23), who is known also from 1 Corinthians 1.14, one cannot be certain that any of these people had been associated with the congregation before the conclusion of Paul's first visit.[4]

Paul's own comment about his Corinthian converts is that "not many" had been "wise by human standards," or "powerful," or "of noble birth" (1 Cor. 1.26, NRSV). This tells us, on the one hand, that the larger number of them were of lower status, both socially and economically. But it also tells us that some *were* persons of con-siderable standing in the eyes of the world. It is probable that the Corinthians whom Paul actually names were among these "not many" of somewhat higher social standing. From what is said about them, they seem to have been well enough off financially to assume positions of civic leadership, to own slaves, to travel, and to

---

[4] In addition to Gaius, four of the people named in Romans 16 seem to have been, by the time of the writing of Romans, members of the Corinthian congregation: Phoebe, a leader of the church in the town of Cenchreae, Corinth's eastern port (16.1); Tertius, who identifies himself as the scribe of the letter (16.22); Erastus, who is described as a city official (16.23); Quartus, who bears a name that was common among slaves and freed-men (16.23).

sponsor house churches.[5] In sum, the Corinthian Christians seem
to have been a very diverse lot, ranging from the very poor to those
of at least moderate wealth, and including persons of differing
social status as well as of various ethnic, religious, and geographical backgrounds.

This diversity doubtless intensified the competition for status
which, reflecting Corinthian society at large, seems from the very
first to have strained relationships among the members of the congregation.[6] Moreover, in this setting the apostle's own status
quickly became an issue. The status-conscious Corinthians were
especially offended by his effort, only partly successful, to support
himself by continuing at his trade (1 Cor. 4.11–12; 9.6; Acts 18.1–4).
In his day it was more socially acceptable for a teacher to earn a
living by charging fees, by dependency on some wealthy patron, or
even by begging.[7] Paul, however, refused to accept financial
support from the Corinthians, even though he claimed the right to
it (1 Cor. 9.3–18), and even though he did accept help from the
Macedonians (2 Cor. 11.8–9). He was thus perceived as demeaning
both himself and the congregation (2 Cor. 11.7, 10–11; 12.13–15).
Later, when he was trying to get the Corinthians to contribute to a
relief fund for the church in Jerusalem, he was even suspected of
raising money under false pretenses (2 Cor. 12.16–18).

Paul's letters to the church

It is certain that Paul wrote at least three letters to his Corinthian
congregation. In addition to the two that have been handed down
as 1 and 2 Corinthians there is the one that he himself mentions in
1 Corinthians 5.9: "I wrote to you in the letter not to associate with
sexually immoral persons." This matter-of-fact reference to "the

---

[5] For important discussions of the social and economic status of Paul's converts, especially
in Corinth, see Gerd Theissen, *The Social Setting of Pauline Christianity: Essays on Corinth*
(Philadelphia, 1982), 69–119; Abraham J. Malherbe, *Social Aspects of Early Christianity* (2nd
edn.; Philadelphia, 1983), 71–91; Wayne A. Meeks, *The First Urban Christians: The Social
World of the Apostle Paul* (New Haven, CT, 1983), 51–73; and Clarke, *Secular and Christian
Leadership in Corinth*.

[6] See especially, Theissen, *Social Setting*, 121–74, and Clarke, *Secular and Christian Leadership in
Corinth*, 59–107.

[7] See Ronald Hock, *The Social Context of Paul's Ministry: Tentmaking and Apostleship*
(Philadelphia, 1980), 52–59.

letter" makes it likely that it was the only one he had sent to Corinth prior to 1 Corinthians. Paul has mentioned it only because he wants to clarify the one particular directive it contained about sexually immoral people; he meant those *within* the church, he says, not those outside (1 Cor. 5.10–11). In order to avoid confusion, the letter described in 1 Corinthians 5.9 may be designated as *Letter A*, and 1 Corinthians itself as *Letter B*.

Some scholars believe that a fragment of Letter A survives in 2 Corinthians 6.14–7.1,[8] yet the evidence for this is meager and the arguments advanced to support it are fragile.[9] It is best to consider this earliest of Paul's Corinthian letters as lost. Because so little is known about its contents, nothing can be said about its overall purpose, where it was written, or its specific date. We know only that Paul must have sent it sometime between his departure from Corinth in 51 (perhaps mid-summer) and his writing of 1 Corinthians (probably in 54 or 55; see below).

In 2 Corinthians, as well as in 1 Corinthians, Paul refers to a letter that he has previously sent to the congregation. He describes this one as having been written "out of an exceedingly troubled, anguished heart" and with "many tears" (2.4). Its purpose had been to enlist the congregation's support in bringing closure to the case of one of their number who had in some respect wronged Paul, and thus the congregation as a whole (2.3, 5–11; 7.8, 12). The long-held view that the letter in question is 1 Corinthians no longer has many defenders.[10] A more widely accepted hypothesis is that this "tearful" (or "severe") letter was written after a second, "painful visit" to Corinth (see 2 Cor. 2.1), and therefore after 1 Corinthians. A number of scholars have argued that this letter (which we may designate as *Letter C*) consisted, at least in part, of what eventually became chapters 10–13 of 2 Corinthians.[11] But

---

8 E.g., John Coolidge Hurd, Jr., *The Origin of I Corinthians* (London, 1965), 235–39.

9 Furnish, *II Corinthians*, 379–80.

10 One of the few is Philip Edgcumbe Hughes, *Paul's Second Epistle to the Corinthians*, NICNT (Grand Rapids, 1962), 63–65.

11 Among the proponents of this view: James Houghton Kennedy, *The Second and Third Epistles of St. Paul to the Corinthians* (London, 1900), 79–94; Alfred Plummer, *A Critical and Exegetical Commentary on the Second Epistle of St Paul to the Corinthians*, ICC (Edinburgh, 1915), xxvii–xxxvi; Günther Bornkamm, "Die Vorgeschichte des sogennanten Zweiten Korintherbriefes," *Gesammelte Aufsätze*, IV, BEvT 53 (Munich, 1971), 172–75; Francis Watson, "2 Cor. x–xiii and Paul's Painful Letter to the Corinthians," *JTS* 35 (1984), 324–46.

another common view is that Letter C, like Letter A, did not survive.[12]

How many other letters Paul may have written to Corinth depends, in part, on whether one holds that 2 Corinthians is a single letter or a composite of two or more originally separate letters. While there are a few scholars who defend the literary integrity of 2 Corinthians,[13] the majority regard at least chapters 10–13 as a separate letter;[14] and there are a number who argue that three (or four) distinct letters can be identified just within chapters 1–9.[15] But however many letters were eventually combined to form 2 Corinthians as it now stands, probably all of them had been written after 1 Corinthians. They therefore reflect developments in Paul's dealings with the church that are subsequent to the letter with which we are here primarily concerned.[16]

Corinthian Christianity

Even though Paul was the first to preach the gospel in Corinth, once a congregation had been founded there it seems to have taken

[12] In addition to Furnish, *II Corinthians*, 159–60, see, especially, Ralph P. Martin, *2 Corinthians*, WBC 40 (Waco, TX, 1986), xlvii–l, and Margaret E. Thrall, *A Critical and Exegetical Commentary on the Second Epistle to the Corinthians*, ICC (Edinburgh, 1994), I.57–61.

[13] E.g., Donald Guthrie, *New Testament Introduction* (3rd edn.; London, 1970), 430–39, 449; Hughes, *Paul's Second Epistle*, xxi–xxxv; Niels Hyldahl, "Die Frage nach der literarischen Einheit des Zweiten Korintherbriefes," *ZNW* 64 (1973), 289–306; Christian Wolff, *Der zweite Brief des Paulus an die Korinther*, THKNT 8 (Berlin, 1970), 1–3.

[14] E.g., Hans Windisch, *Der zweite Korintherbrief*, KEK (9th edn.; Göttingen, 1924 [repr. edited by Georg Strecker, 1970]), 11–21; C. K. Barrett, *A Commentary on the Second Epistle to the Corinthians*, BNTC (London, 1973), 11–21; Furnish, *II Corinthians*, 35–48; Martin, *2 Corinthians*, xxxviii–lii; Thrall, *Second Epistle*, 5–20.

[15] E.g., Bornkamm, "Vorgeschichte," 186–87; Hans-Martin Schenke and Karl Martin Fischer, *Einleitung in die Schriften des Neuen Testaments. I: Die Briefe des Paulus und Schriften des Paulinismus* (Gütersloh, 1978), 109–12; Helmut Koester, *Introduction to the New Testament*, II: *History and Literature of Early Christianity*, Hermeneia: Foundations and Facets (Philadelphia, 1982), 127–30, 136–37; Hans Dieter Betz, *2 Corinthians 8 and 9. A Commentary on Two Administrative Letters of the Apostle Paul*, Hermeneia (Philadelphia, 1985), 142–43.

[16] In my view (*II Corinthians*, 35–48), chs. 1–9 (or at least chs. 1–8) are to be identified as *Letter D* (written from Macedonia, perhaps in the fall of 55), and chs. 10–13 with *Letter E* (also from Macedonia, perhaps in the spring or summer of 56); cf. the scholars named in n. 14, above; also Jerome Murphy-O'Connor, *The Theology of the Second Letter to the Corinthians*, New Testament Theology (Cambridge, 1991), 16–17. All of the scholars named in n. 15 identify at least three letters in 2 Corinthians, in the following sequence: (1) 2.14–6.13 + 7.2–4; (2) chs. 10–13; (3) 1.1–2.13 + 7.5–16 (+ 13.11–13); but these scholars differ in their judgments about chs. 8 and 9.

on a life of its own. To be sure, its founding apostle continued to exercise significant pastoral direction by means of the letters he wrote, the representatives he sent, and his own subsequent visits. But other forces were also at work shaping Corinthian Christianity. From several remarks by Paul himself we know that Apollos must have been teaching in Corinth within the first few years of the congregation's founding (1 Cor. 3.6; 16.12), and that he had made a lasting impression on the congregation (1 Cor. 1.12; 3.4–5, 22; 4.6). Cephas, too, seems to have had a following there (1 Cor 1.12; 3.22), although nothing Paul says suggests that Cephas himself had ever been in Corinth. It is possible, however, that others from the Jerusalem church had ministered there as his representatives (see 9.5; 15.5).

In addition to the influences exerted by various itinerating ministers of the gospel, Corinthian Christianity was quite evidently shaped by the diverse cultural, social, religious, and political currents and institutions that made up its urban environment. To be sure, Paul expresses confidence that his converts had abandoned certain of their former practices (1 Cor. 6.9–11), and it is clear that they would have experienced at least the disruption, and often the total alteration, of their relationships to family, friends, and society at large. Yet the apostle also recognizes that believers cannot separate themselves entirely from society (e.g., 1 Cor. 5.9–10; 7.12–13), and that conversion marks only the beginning of their acculturation to the gospel (1 Cor. 3.1–3). As a consequence, Paul's task was not only to help his congregation define itself in relation to "the world" outside. His equally urgent and perhaps more difficult task was to help it reckon with that world as it continued to be present in the lives of believers, and therefore within the church itself. Especially in the ways they related to one another and to their leaders (including Paul), and in certain of their congregational structures and practices, the Corinthian Christians continued to be influenced by the social patterns and conventions of Roman Corinth.[17]

Because our only source for the theological views prevailing in the congregation is the apostle himself, all characterizations of

---

[17] For particulars: Clarke, *Secular and Christian Leadership in Corinth*; Chow, *Patronage and Power*.

those must remain general and provisional. Judging from 1 Corinthians, he was having to contend with understandings of life in Christ that were in certain essential respects at odds with the gospel that he preached.[18]

(1) The Corinthians viewed Jesus mainly as "the Lord of glory" (2.8), and took little or no account of his crucifixion as an event of saving significance.[19]

(2) They understood themselves, as believers, to be the recipients of special religious wisdom and privileged with special knowledge about God (e.g., 4.10; 8.2), and perhaps regarded this as a sign of their own present reigning with Christ in glorious triumph (e.g., 4.8).

(3) They highly valued spiritual gifts, and those who could display extraordinary ones, particularly the gift of ecstatic utterance (speaking in tongues), thereby advanced their religious standing within the congregation (chapters 12–14).[20]

(4) At least some in the congregation, perhaps because they believed themselves to be sharing already in Christ's glorious reign, had all but ceased to hope for anything beyond this life (15.12–19).

(5) Finally, some, or perhaps even most, of the congregation believed that in reigning with Christ they were delivered from needing to worry with questions of right and wrong, and with distinguishing moral from immoral actions. To characterize this view Paul cited, or perhaps himself devised, the slogan, "Everything is permissible for me" (6.12; 10.23). Others, however, seem to have embraced an almost opposite view, convinced that in reigning with Christ they were required to distance themselves as far as possible from the moral stain of worldly involvements (e.g., sexual relations, as indicated by a

---

[18] An especially careful discussion of what can and cannot be known about Corinthian Christianity is provided by Wolfgang Schrage, *Der erste Brief an die Korinther*, EKKNT 7 (Zürich/Braunschweig/Neukirchen-Vluyn, 1991 [pt. I], 1995 [pt. II]), I.38–63.

[19] Paul's reference to the *crucifixion* of "the Lord of glory" implicitly corrects the Corinthian view by accentuating the paradox of the cross. In Jewish apocalyptic circles, God was sometimes described as "the Lord of glory" (*1 Enoch* 22.14; 25.3; 63.2). It is impossible to know whether the phrase was actually employed as a christological title in Corinth. It does not appear elsewhere in Paul's letters.

[20] See Dale B. Martin, *The Corinthian Body* (New Haven, CT, 1995), 87–103.

statement Paul quotes from a letter the church had written to
him, 7.1b).

Summarized formally, in terms of traditional theological categories, the prevailing Corinthian interpretation of the gospel had
departed from Paul's own interpretation of it in four critical
respects: christologically, by taking little or no account of Jesus'
death; soteriologically, by misconstruing the meaning of one's
freedom in Christ; eschatologically, by failing to appreciate the
apostle's dialectical understanding of salvation, as both "already"
and "not yet"; and ecclesiologically, by neglecting the corporate
dimension of life in Christ.

APPROACHING I CORINTHIANS

Although 1 Corinthians is a profoundly theological document, it
has to be approached and read as the letter it is, not as a theological essay. It was called forth by particular circumstances and
addressed to a specific situation. Moreover, in composing it Paul
followed many of the rhetorical and epistolary conventions of his
day. Therefore, before proceeding with an examination of theology in 1 Corinthians, it is imperative that we give some attention to
the letter's situational orientation, specific aims, and overall structure. Although the literary integrity of 1 Corinthians has not gone
unchallenged,[21] most scholars do not find the various partition the-
ories either persuasive or necessary.[22] The unity of the letter may
therefore be assumed, even though the presence of occasional edi-
torial interpolations is not to be ruled out.[23]

[21] Thus Robert Jewett, "The Redaction of I Corinthians and the Trajectory of the Pauline School," *JAAR* 44, Supplement B (1978), 389–444; Gerhard Sellin, "Hauptprobleme des ersten Korintherbriefes," *ANRW* 2.25.4 (ed. by H. Temporini and W. Haase; Berlin and New York, 1987), 2940–3044; idem, "I Korinther 5–6 und der 'Vorbrief' nach Korinth: Indizien für eine Mehrschichtigkeit von Kommunikationsakten im ersten Korintherbrief," *NTS* 37 (1991), 535–58.

[22] See, e.g., Werner Georg Kümmel, *Introduction to the New Testament* (rev. edn.; Nashville and New York, 1975), 275–78; Helmut Merklein, "Die Einheitlichkeit des ersten Korintherbriefes," *Studien zu Jesus und Paulus*, WUNT 2/43 (Tübingen, 1987), 345–75; Schrage, *Der erste Brief*, I.63–71; John C. Hurd, "Good News and the Integrity of 1 Corinthians," *Gospel in Paul: Studies on Corinthians, Galatians and Romans for Richard N. Longenecker*, JSNTSup 108 (ed. by L. Ann Jervis and Peter Richardson; Sheffield, 1994), 38–62.

[23] The most likely instance of a post-Pauline interpolation is the instruction in 14.34–35 that women should be "silent in the churches" and "subordinate, as the law also says." For

Occasion and aims

It is evident that 1 Corinthians was written in Ephesus, where Paul was intending to remain, along with Sosthenes (1 Cor. 1.1), until the following Pentecost (16.8). The year was most likely either 54 or 55.[24] The apostle planned, after Pentecost, to go to Macedonia and then on to Corinth, where he would spend the following winter (16.5–7). Meanwhile, Timothy had already been sent out from Ephesus toward Corinth (4.17). Because Paul anticipated that his letter would be received there before Timothy's arrival (16.10), it is likely that the letter was to be carried by someone who would be sailing directly to Corinth, while Timothy had been sent overland, presumably by way of Macedonia. In any event, one of Paul's reasons for writing this letter was to commend Timothy and the counsels that he would be imparting (16.10–11; cf. 4.17). Another reason for writing was to impress upon the congregation the need to be prepared for his own coming. For one thing, Paul wanted the Corinthians to be ready with their contribution for the offering that he was collecting for the Jerusalem Christians (16.1–4). For another, he was hoping to find evidence that they had taken seriously his appeals, conveyed in this letter and also by way of Timothy, to conduct themselves in accord with the gospel that they had received (4.14–21).

There were certainly plenty of things going on in Corinth to cause Paul concern. He would have gotten wind of at least some of these in a letter, apparently written on behalf of the whole congregation, which must have asked whether sexual relationships were ever proper for Christians (7.1). It is possible, but not certain, that this same letter prompted Paul's comments on three further issues: whether believers were allowed to eat meat from animals that had been ceremonially slaughtered for pagan rites (8.1–11.1);

the relevant evidence and arguments see Gordon D. Fee, *The First Epistle to the Corinthians*, NICNT (Grand Rapids, 1987), 699–708, and *God's Empowering Presence: The Holy Spirit in the Letters of Paul* (Peabody, MA, 1994), 272–81.

[24] For the evidence in support of this general dating see, e.g., Robert Jewett, *A Chronology of Paul's Life* (Philadelphia, 1979), 95–104, and Schrage, *Der erste Brief*, I.36–38. Not many have been persuaded by the arguments made for an earlier dating, in 49 or 52, by Gerd Luedemann, *Paul, Apostle to the Gentiles: Studies in Chronology* (Philadelphia, 1984), 162–94 and 262–63.

whether certain spiritual gifts, above all, ecstatic speech, were to be particularly coveted and honored (chapters 12–14); and how the congregation was to fulfill the pledge it had made to Paul's collection for the Jerusalem church (16.1–4).[25]

The most troubling news, perhaps, had been conveyed to Paul by word of mouth. He identifies "Chloe's people" as having reported on certain factions that were emerging within the church (1.11–12), perhaps as one result of competing claims about Christian baptism and spiritual wisdom (1.13–17). From these same people, or others, the apostle had also learned that the congregation was arrogantly indifferent to a specific case of sexual immorality in its midst (5.1–2). And he had been informed, further, that when the congregation assembled for its community meal, which included the Lord's supper, its neediest members were being marginalized and allowed to go hungry while others were overindulging themselves with food and strong drink (11.17–22).

In addition to these problems, some members of the church were beginning to raise questions about Paul's apostolic status and authority. The partisan slogans that he cites in 1.12 ("I am Paul's," "I am Apollos'," etc.) are symptomatic of this, and his comments in chapter 9 about his apostolic policies are offered, in part, as a response to those who are critical of how he has conducted himself (see, especially, 9.1–3). Those critics must also be in mind when Paul remarks that only God's judgment about his ministry counts, not the judgment of human beings (4.3; cf. 10.29–30), and then again when he concedes that he had been an unlikely prospect for apostleship, and that the risen Christ had appeared to him "last of all" (15.8–11).

To sum up: 1 Corinthians was written in response both to a letter that Paul had received from his congregation and to word-of-mouth reports that he had received about it. While he therefore discusses various issues on which his counsel has been specifically requested, he also addresses some matters about which his counsel has not been sought, at least not in writing. Moreover, and even

---

[25] Although the same Greek formula (*peri de,* "Now concerning") is employed in 7.1; 8.1; 12.1 and 16.1 (and again in 16.12), a reference to the Corinthians' letter is coupled with it only in the first instance. When the formula is used by itself, as in the subsequent instances, it offers no basis for inferring the existence of a letter. See Margaret M. Mitchell, "Concerning ΠΕΡΙ ΔΕ in 1 Corinthians," *NovT* 31 (1989), 229–56.

more important, Paul is concerned throughout this letter to reaffirm his understanding of the gospel, and to reaffirm the authority by which he had first preached it to the Corinthians and seeks now to interpret it for them.

Genre, structure, and style

It is easy enough to identify 1 Corinthians as a letter, both in form and in function, but several additional points need to be registered about its literary genre. First, along with virtually all of Paul's letters (Philemon is the exception), it is to be associated with letters of a semi-literary type. That is, it does not just communicate a few pieces of specific information or attest one particular fact, but discusses at some length various topics of concern to the writer. Second, it is addressed not just to an individual or to a few people (e.g., a family), but to an entire congregation, with the expectation that upon its receipt it will be read out for all to hear. Third, it is written by one who claims to exercise special authority over those he addresses, partly because he is the founder of the congregation to which they belong, but even more fundamentally because he understands himself to have been divinely commissioned to preach the gospel. Thus 1 Corinthians is written as an *apostolic* letter, and this in itself sets it apart within its genre.

There have been numerous attempts to identify 1 Corinthians with one or another of the letter *types* discussed by ancient epistolary theorists.[26] These attempts have run into difficulties, however, because typologies varied somewhat from one theorist to another, and because the categories set up even within one typology are often overlapping. Thus, while 1 Corinthians can be generally described as *a letter of exhortation and advice*, little is gained by trying to identify it with some precise sub-type within this larger category.[27]

---

[26] Representative passages from these theorists have been assembled and translated by Abraham J. Malherbe, *Ancient Epistolary Theorists*, SBLSBS 19 (Atlanta, 1988).

[27] The category, "letters of exhortation and advice," is employed and discussed by Stanley K. Stowers, *Letter-Writing in Greco-Roman Antiquity*, Library of Early Christianity, 5 (Philadelphia, 1986), 91–152. The most successful attempt at greater precision is that by Margaret M. Mitchell, who regards 1 Corinthians as an advisory letter of the specifically *deliberative* type; see *Paul and the Rhetoric of Reconciliation. An Exegetical Investigation of the Language and Composition of 1 Corinthians*, HUT 28 (Tübingen, 1992; repr. Louisville, KY, 1993), especially 20–64.

The overall structure of 1 Corinthians conforms by and large to other Hellenistic letters of the semi-literary type. Following the mandatory epistolary prescript, which identifies the letter's writer(s) and recipients (1.1–3), there is an introductory paragraph, in this case (which is typical for Paul) a thanksgiving (1.4–9). The body of the letter, which both begins and ends with an appeal, extends from 1.10 through 15.58. Finally, a rather lengthy epistolary postscript includes instructions about the collection for Jerusalem (16.1–4), information about the travel plans of Paul, Timothy, and Apollos, respectively (16.5–12), a few summary appeals and counsels (16.13–18), greetings (16.19–20), and a subscript penned by Paul himself, which includes a benediction (16.21–24).

The structure of the argument in 1 Corinthians has been variously delineated, and it is probably wise to resist fastening on any one particular analysis as definitive. However, the body of the letter can be divided fairly readily into four main sections.[28]

In the first of these, 1.10–4:21, Paul issues a call for unity in the congregation, arguing that the rivalries and competition for status with which the Corinthians have been preoccupied do not accord with the gospel on which their faith is founded. Because he has learned of partisan claims about himself and Apollos, especially, he stresses that all servants of the gospel have equal standing and are equally accountable before God (3.5–15). However, this does not prompt him to yield any ground to Apollos' Corinthian partisans. Instead, he supports his appeals for unity by claiming special authority as the congregation's founding apostle, by mentioning Timothy's impending visit as his representative, and by warning that things had better improve before his own visit later on (4.14–21).

In one way or another, the issues taken up in the second section, 5.1–11.1, all derive from the church's struggle to *be* the church in a world to which it does not finally belong. Here Paul directs that an incestuous man be put out of the church (5.1–13), counsels against suing any fellow believer in the pagan courts (6.1–11), and warns believers about getting involved in improper sexual relationships

---

[28] A similar analysis, although differing in details, is offered by Mitchell, *Paul and the Rhetoric of Reconciliation*, 184–86 (synopsis) and 186–295 (discussion).

(6.12–20). Subsequently, he comments on various questions that the Corinthians have raised with him about marriage and divorce, including the propriety of believers remaining married to unbelievers (7.1–40). He then goes on to point out what believers must consider in deciding whether to eat meat that has come from pagan rites (8.1–11.1).

The counsels in the third section, 11.2–14.40, provide guidance on how the Corinthian Christians should conduct themselves when they are assembled as a congregation. First, there are instructions about how women who prophesy in the assembly should arrange their hair (11.3–16). These are followed by some particularly earnest counsels and solemn warnings about the congregation's common meal, during which it is customary for believers to share in a ritual loaf and cup (11.17–34). Finally, there are extended comments on how the Corinthians' vaunted spiritual gifts are to be estimated, and several specific directives for maintaining order in the assembly while these are being exercised (12.1–14.40).

The body of the letter is concluded in chapter 15, where Paul responds to those in the congregation who are denying that there is any resurrection of the dead (15.12). He first cites the tradition about Christ's own death and resurrection on which their faith is based (15.1–11). As he then proceeds with his main argument (15.12–34), he posits the further, critical point that Christ has been raised from the dead as "the first fruits of those who have fallen asleep" (15.20). The discussion continues with comments about the nature of the resurrection body (15.35–49) and the mystery of transformation (15.50–56), and closes with an expression of thanksgiving (15.57) and a pastoral appeal (15.58).

In addressing these various matters, the apostle has employed many of the same stylistic conventions and rhetorical strategies that are present in other ancient letters of exhortation and advice. First Corinthians contains both specific directives (e.g., 5.4–5; ch. 7; 14.27–31) and general appeals (e.g., 10.31; 14.20, 40; 15.58), both commendations (e.g., 11.2) and reprimands (e.g., 6.5; 11.17–22), both promises (e.g., 6.14) and threats (e.g., 3.17–18; 4.19–21). Here one finds the use of examples (including that of Paul's own life and conduct, e.g., 4.14–17; 8.13; 10.32–11.1), citations from authorities (Scripture, e.g., 1.31; 14.21; Jesus' teachings, 7.10–11; 9.14; Christian traditions, e.g., 15.3–5), and appeals to the hearers' own experience (e.g., 1.26–31; 6.11), reason (e.g., 10.15; 11.13), "nature" (11.14–15), custom (11.16), and plain common sense (e.g., 5.10; 9.7).

There are, in addition, numerous expository statements and several expository passages in 1 Corinthians. These are especially important for students of Paul's thought. For example, he often accompanies a citation of Scripture or of some church tradition with a comment intended to clarify or elaborate its meaning. Even his glossing of cited materials, in so far as this can be detected, is a form of exposition. But his exposition is not only tied to specific citations. It is present wherever the apostle has developed and presented his thoughts in a way calculated to inform or edify his congregation. These expository statements and passages will require special attention as we seek to determine the theological orientation of 1 Corinthians.

Points of reference

Even as Romans is generally considered the most theological of Paul's letters, so 1 Corinthians is commonly regarded as one of his most practical. Yet the apostle himself seems to have discerned that the pastoral problems with which he was faced in Corinth were but symptoms of an underlying misunderstanding of his gospel. Therefore, in dealing with those problems he repeatedly calls on his hearers to consider what the gospel has accomplished among them, and how, when it is faithfully received, the gospel wholly redefines and reshapes believers' lives. It is in this connection that we meet Paul the theologian even in 1 Corinthians – identifying what he understands to constitute the gospel, explicating its truth, and commenting on what it entails.

Within the developing argument of this letter, and in the theological exposition that is integral to it, there are three special points of reference. One is Scripture, which for the apostle and his churches was the Septuagint, a Greek version of the Hebrew Bible (expanded with some other writings) that was part of Christianity's Hellenistic-Jewish heritage. Another is the church's developing fund of traditional materials and formulations – confessional, liturgical, and the like. The third, of a very different order, is Paul's own sense of apostolic vocation. It will serve our understanding of theology in 1 Corinthians if, before proceeding any farther, we give some attention to each of these special points of reference, and also to the place and character of theological exposition in this letter.

Scripture

In 1 Corinthians, as in his other letters, Scripture is a reference point for Paul's thinking about the gospel in two respects. The less obvious of these is, arguably, the more important. During the course of his upbringing and life as a Jew he had been steeped in knowledge of his people's sacred texts and profoundly formed, both in his thinking and in his conduct, by traditional ways of reading and interpreting them. Still as a Christian, he is a person who has been formed in fundamental ways by the Jewish Scripture and traditions. In 1 Corinthians, this heritage is apparent in much of what Paul presupposes and affirms about God and God's creation, including humankind, and frequently in the ways he expresses himself about these. Indeed, specific scriptural themes and points of view are often present even where no scriptural text is cited. Thus throughout this letter, Scripture remains an *implicit* point of reference.

There are also places in 1 Corinthians where Scripture is an *explicit* point of reference, invoked as a special authority (thus 1 Cor. 9.8). In a number of instances Paul actually quotes from it, more often than not introducing the quotation(s) in a way that indicates a scriptural origin.[29] Some of the quotations closely correspond to textual traditions known to us, while others diverge from those. In two cases the apostle glosses the quoted material with his own point (15.26, 45b), and sometimes he appends an explanatory comment (9.9b–10; 15.27b, 46–47, 56). He has drawn quotations, about equally, from all three parts of the traditional Hellenistic-Jewish canon – the Law,[30] the Prophets,[31] and the

---

[29] The most elaborate of his introductory statements are in 9.9 ("For in the law of Moses it stands written . . .") and 15.54 ("the saying that stands written will come to pass . . .").

[30] Gen. 2.7, in 15.45; Gen. 2.24, in 6.16; Exod. 32.6, in 10.7; Deut. 17.7, in 5.13; Deut. 25.4, in 9.9.

[31] Isa. 22.13, in 15.27; Isa. 25.7 (combined with Hos. 13.14), in 15.54; Isa. 28.11–12, in 14.21; Isa. 29.14, in 1.19; Isa. 40.13, in 2.16; Jer. 9.24, in 1.31. Some hold that the quotation in 1 Cor. 1.31 derives from 1 Samuel rather than Jeremiah, but the latter is more likely, given the echoes of Jer. 9.23–24 in 1 Cor. 1.27–28. The commentaries provide details.

Writings.[32] Perhaps contrary to expectations, he quotes Scripture only three times in connection with his moral counsels (6.16; 10.7; 10.26) and, again, only three times in connection with his directives about church policies and practices (5.13; 9.9; 14.21). Specific quotations appear more often in the course of exposition – near the beginning of the letter where his topic is wisdom (1.19, 31; 2.9, 16; 3.19–20), and near its close where his topic is resurrection (15.25, 27, 32, 45, 54–55).

Elsewhere in 1 Corinthians there are clear, sometimes extended allusions to scriptural passages that are not actually quoted, as in 11.7–12 where the Genesis creation accounts are in view. A particularly notable instance is 10.1–22. There Paul supports his admonition to flee idolatry (10.14) with examples, drawn especially from Exodus and Numbers, of the punishment that Israel had suffered for her apostasy. His remark that Israel's experiences "were written down to be a warning for us, on whom the ends of the ages have come" (10.11), is especially important. The reference to "the ends of the ages" reflects the point of view from which Paul assesses and interprets Scripture. It is the point of view of one who is in Christ, and who perceives that all of the past epochs of human history (see 2.7) are now coming to an end (cf. 2 Esd. 11.44). When he claims that Scripture was written "for us" (see 1 Cor. 9.10 as well as 10.11), he does not mean that it is the key to understanding Christ. For him the reverse is true: Christ is the key to the interpretation of Scripture. It is "for us" in the sense that its deepest meaning is evident only to the believing community (see also 2 Cor. 3.7–4.6).[33]

As a consequence, although Scripture is one of Paul's important points of reference in 1 Corinthians, it is the gospel, not Scripture, that informs his counsels, is the subject of his exposition, and shapes his argument.[34] He may regard Scripture as an important

---

[32] Ps. 8.6, in 15.27; Ps. 24.1, in 10.26; Ps. 94[Greek, 93].11 (combined with Job 5.12–13), in 3.20; Ps. 110.1, in 15.25. Although the quotation in 1 Cor. 2.9 is introduced as scriptural, an exact source has not been identified (but see Isa. 64.4). The vague, almost gratuitous reference to Scripture in 14.34 ("as the law says, too") is unique in the Pauline letters, and is one reason for suspecting that the instruction about women in 14.34–35 is a later, non-Pauline interpolation (see above, n. 23).

[33] For further comments on 1 Cor. 10.11, see the important study by Richard B. Hays, *Echoes of Scripture in the Letters of Paul* (New Haven, CT, and London, 1989), 99–102, 168–69.

[34] Contrast the judgment of Brian Rosner, whose study of 1 Corinthians 5–7 leads him to conclude that, at least for Paul's ethics, "the Scriptures are . . . a crucial and formative

witness to the gospel, and in its own way a manifestation of it. But for Paul, the definitive manifestation of the gospel is Jesus Christ, whom he has come to know in the church's traditions and, decisively, through the revelation that constituted his call to apostleship.

Church traditions

Traditions are vital to a community's functioning, and most especially to the functioning of religious communities. The traditions of a religious community constitute its corporate memory, and as such are a primary means by which the beliefs, expectations, and practices that warrant its existence are continually nourished, critiqued, and renewed. The church's traditions were functioning in these ways from its earliest years, and were an important part of Paul's specifically Christian heritage. Because the church's traditions were predominantly oral, it is harder than in the case of Scripture to detect where he depends on them. Nonetheless, almost all of his letters contain clear signs of such dependence.

In 1 Corinthians, for example, there are four instances where the apostle introduces material in a way that marks it as traditional. He identifies both the prohibition of divorce (7.10–11) and a rule about living expenses for those who preach the gospel (9.14) as commanded by "the Lord," showing that he has access to some collection of *dominical sayings*.[35] A third dominical saying, which associates Jesus' body and blood with the ritual loaf and cup shared by his followers (11.23b–25), may come from the church's *liturgical* tradition. The idiom that Paul uses in introducing it, "received . . . handed on" (11.23a), regularly signals the presence of traditional material. He uses this idiom again when introducing a statement about Christ's death and resurrection (15.3–5), which must have had a place within the church's *confessional* tradition.

There are five additional places in 1 Corinthians where Paul

---

source . . ." (*Paul's Scripture and Ethics: A Study of 1 Corinthians 5–7*, AGJU 22 [Leiden, 1994], 24).

[35] Similar versions of these traditional sayings appear, respectively, in Mark 10.2–12 (divorce) and Luke 10.7 (living expenses). For further comments on these passages and the topic in general, see V. P. Furnish, *Jesus According to Paul*, Understanding Jesus Today (Cambridge, 1993), 40–65, and the much more detailed and technical study by Frans J. Neirynck, "Paul and the Sayings of Jesus," in *L'Apôtre Paul: Personnalité, style et conception du ministère*, BETL 73 (ed. by A. Vanhoye; Leuven, 1986), 265–321.

seems to have incorporated traditional material. Other confessional formulations are identifiable in 6.11 (affirming deliverance from an old way of life), in 8.6 (affirming "one God" and "one Lord"), and in 12.3 (affirming Jesus as "Lord"). A prayer in 16.22, left in Aramaic (*marana tha*, "Our Lord, come!"), had probably been part of the liturgical tradition of the church since its earliest years in Jerusalem. And a warning in 6.9–10 (about those who will not inherit God's kingdom) is representative of the church's *parenetic* tradition, an eclectic stock of moral advice. In all of these places, traditional materials have been taken over more or less intact. There are yet other places where one finds fragments or echoes of traditional formulations, especially of the confessional type (1.30; 5.7b; 6.14a, 20a; 7.23; 8.11; 12.13).

Most of the traditions that are employed or echoed in this letter have either a specifically christological focus or a significant christological component. In three of the places where this obtains, 8.6, 11.23b–25, and 15.3b–5, the tradition employed is a particularly important point of reference for Paul as he lays out his thinking and makes his appeals. The same can be said of the statement in 12.13 about baptism "into one body," which echoes a confessional formula that is probably more intact in Galatians 3.27–28 (cf. Col. 3.11).

Both from these passages and from the letter as a whole it is clear that Paul's thinking about the gospel is informed by the church's traditions and frequently in dialogue with them. However, it is also clear that the traditions do not, collectively, *constitute* his gospel or dominate his thinking about it. Unquestionably, they remain a special point of reference for him; but no less certainly, he remains their interpreter.

Apostolic vocation

Paul was not a detached interpreter of the gospel. He proclaimed and served it as one who had himself been profoundly changed by its saving power. Later generations would refer to his "conversion," but Paul himself seems not to have distinguished that, at least in retrospect, from his call to apostleship. This is particularly evident from the remarks he makes in Galatians 1.11–17, to the effect that the revelation to him of God's Son was for the purpose and had the result of his proclaiming Christ among the Gentiles (Gal. 1.16). The same connection between his encounter with Christ and his call to apostleship is present in 1 Corinthians 9.1–2 (he has seen the Lord and is an apostle "at least" to the Corinthians) and 15.8–10 (the resurrected Christ appeared also to him, "the least" of the apostles).

Paul opens 1 Corinthians, as he does most of his letters, by presenting himself as an apostle – in this case, "of Christ Jesus, by God's will" (1.1). By thus identifying himself, he is also asserting the authority with which he writes and that he intends his congregation to respect. In a general way, therefore, Paul's sense of apostolic vocation is an implicit point of reference throughout the letter. And there are several places, although fewer than one might expect, where he specifically invokes his apostolic authority (7.25, 40; cf. 4.15).

Paul's sense of apostolic vocation is a particularly significant point of reference in three distinct sections of 1 Corinthians. The first of these is 1.10–4.21, where he decries the partisan and competing claims that are being voiced in the congregation about himself and others. In this context Paul's main concern is not to emphasize his own apostolic authority, because that would almost certainly add fuel to the fire. Instead, he argues that all of those whom the Corinthians have been heroizing are equally God's servants, ultimately accountable to the Lord, and that they have been assigned distinctive and complementary tasks (see 3.5–9, 10–17; 4.1–5, 15).

A second and more striking instance is 1 Corinthians 9. After arguing that he has the same right as every other apostle to be provided a living by his churches (9.1–14), he proceeds to explain that he has nevertheless declined to exercise this right lest it hinder the furtherance of the gospel that he has been called to proclaim (9.15–23). It may be that his refusal to accept financial support from the Corinthians had offended them, because in Greco-Roman society one important way of gaining honor and status was to become someone's patron. But within its context (8.1–11.1) the primary function of chapter 9 is to support Paul's counsels about eating meat left over from pagan sacrifices. The principle he wants followed is the one illustrated by his own apostolic practice: where

making use of a right may harm others by leading them into idolatry, that right should not be exercised.

Two of the rhetorical questions with which chapter 9 is introduced are worth special notice. Paul asks, in turn, "Am I not an
apostle? Have I not seen Jesus our Lord?" (9.1, NRSV). The claim
implicit in the second question is meant to validate the claim
implicit in the first. Paul can be an apostle, and is one, because he
has "seen Jesus our Lord." The reference is to a past event that continues to shape his life,[36] unquestionably the same encounter with
Christ that he describes elsewhere as the revelation to him of God's
Son (Gal. 1.15–17). Paul regards that revelation as definitive both of
his apostleship – he is "an apostle of Christ Jesus" (e.g., 1 Cor. 1.1)
– and of the gospel that he has been sent to proclaim, which he
identifies as "the gospel of Christ" (e.g., 1 Cor. 9.12).

This encounter with Christ is mentioned yet again in 1
Corinthians 15, where for the third time in the letter Paul's apostolic vocation is a special point of reference. Here the apostle
boldly presents his seeing of the Lord as incidental to one of the
appearances of the resurrected Christ, albeit the last of them
(15.8–10). As in 9.1 (also in Gal. 1.15–16), he presupposes that his
call to apostleship was intrinsic to his encounter with Christ. And
as in 3.10 (also in Gal. 1.15; 2.9; Rom. 1.5; 12.3; 15.15), he refers to
his apostolic vocation as an act of divine grace. However, his principal objective in this context is not to describe or defend his apostleship, but to remind the Corinthians that the gospel on which
their faith is founded affirms Christ's resurrection from the dead
(15.1–5). The reference to his apostleship is for the purpose of
helping to secure this premise (see 15.11), from which he then proceeds to argue in the remainder of chapter 15.

In sum, Paul was certain that, for himself, there could be no real
belonging to Christ without being Christ's apostle. This conviction
is evident, for example, when he refers to apostleship as an "obli-
gation" laid upon him, and then adds, "Woe to me, if I do not proclaim the gospel!" (1 Cor. 9.16, NRSV). He clearly did not think
that every believer was called to be an apostle (1 Cor. 12.29).
However, he was convinced that his own sharing in the gospel had

---

[36] This is the force of the Greek perfect tense, which Paul has used here ("have . . . seen").

to take the form of obedience to such a call (1 Cor. 9.22–23). As a result, everything that Paul wrote concerning the gospel bears the imprint of his sense of apostolic vocation, and along with that, the imprint of his life-transforming encounter with Christ. But equally important, nothing that he wrote has the form of a merely "personal testimony." And, at least in 1 Corinthians, his theological reflection is never oriented just to what he himself has experienced of God's grace. Especially in 1 Corinthians, he is intent on showing that the saving power of the gospel is simply not reducible to anyone's personal experience of it.

Theological exposition

As we have seen, it is the gospel – not Scripture, the church's tradition, or his own "Christian experience" – that is the primary subject of Paul's theological reflection and exposition in 1 Corinthians. There are a number of specific references to the gospel in this letter, variously phrased and in various contexts.[37] In general, however, these presuppose more than they reveal about the apostle's conception of what the gospel is and means. For this we must turn to the letter's expository statements and passages.

The expository statements in 1 Corinthians are confined, for the most part, to occasional paragraphs, sentences, or even phrases. In some instances theological exposition introduces the moral advice, as when counsels about eating meat from pagan temples are preceded by comments about knowledge and love and statements about the one God and the one Lord (8.1–6). Typically, however, theological exposition stands within the appeals and is integral to them. For example, in chapter 7 instructions about marriage and divorce are supported by reflections, first, on the consequences of God's call for one's present situation in society (7.17–24), and then on the passing away of this present age (7.29–31). Further examples are offered by 3.1–4.5, where warnings about partisanship are hardly separable from comments about God's servants, worldly

---

[37] There are references to "the gospel" (*to euangelion*, 4.15; 9.12, 14, 18, 23; 15.1) and "preaching the gospel" (*euangelizesthai*, 1.17; 9.16, 18; 15.1, 2), to "the proclamation" (*to kērygma*, 1.21; 2.4; 15.14) and "proclaiming" (*kēryssein*, 1.23; 9.27; 15.11, 12), and to "the word of the cross" (1.18; cf. "my word," 2.4) and "the word of God" (14.36).

wisdom, and belonging to Christ, and by 6.12–20, where the appeal to "distance yourselves from sexual immorality" is supported by statements about God's raising of the dead, the Lord's claim on one's body, and one's body being a "temple" for the Holy Spirit.

In addition, however, there are three longer expository passages, each one located prominently and strategically within the argument of the letter. The first (1.18–2.16) is in the opening section where Paul is urging his congregation to manifest the unity that is proper to those who are truly in Christ. The second (12.12–13.13) occurs as he begins his discussion of spiritual gifts. The third (15:1–58) concludes the body of the letter, thereby helping to undergird all of the preceding appeals and counsels. The topics of these expositions are, respectively, the wisdom of the cross, the believing community, and the resurrection of the dead. In each of them the apostle is concerned to set forth his reflection on the truth of the gospel and his understanding of how the gospel ought to be shaping the congregation's faith and life. In this general sense these three passages are authentically *theological* discourses.

The theological orientation of these passages is representative of the theological orientation of the letter as a whole. They are all *soteriologically* oriented, because in each of them Paul is presupposing his own and the believing community's participation in God's new creation. They are all *christologically* oriented, because in each of them he views Christ as the one in whom God's saving power and purpose are definitively revealed and active. They are all *eschatologically* oriented, because in each of them he is looking beyond this present, passing age to the larger and ultimate reality of God's final victory. And they are all *ecclesiologically* oriented, because in each of them Paul is presupposing the view that he expresses quite specifically with his metaphor of the church as a body: the present, saving reality of life in Christ must be actualized always, and ever anew, in the life of a faithful community as well as in the lives of faithful individuals.

It is, of course, no coincidence that this fourfold theological orientation of the letter corresponds to Paul's estimate of how the gospel was being misunderstood in Corinth.[38] However, it would

---

[38] Above, 9–12.

be a mistake to approach 1 Corinthians as if it could yield soterio-logical, christological, eschatological, and ecclesiological concepts. Paul did not have ready-made theological bandages to apply to Corinthian wounds. His thinking did not proceed according to formal categories like these. A better approach, because it accords with the context and character of the apostle's theological reflection, is to follow his own line of thought through the four major sections of the letter. This will keep us in touch with the set-tings, both epistolary and situational, within which his affirmations and expositions of the gospel actually functioned, while still allow-ing us to give particular attention to his theological reflection.

CHAPTER 2

Knowing God, belonging to Christ

The first four chapters of 1 Corinthians contain some important clues about the practical situation in the Corinthian congregation, and also provide examples of Paul's considerable skill as a rhetorical strategist. They are no less important, however, for what they disclose about the overall theological orientation of this letter.[1] In particular, the apostle's comments about knowing God (e.g., 1.21; 2.8, 11, 14) and belonging to Christ (e.g., 1.9; 3.23) introduce themes that are also prominent in succeeding sections.

As regards the first of these, it is worth noting that the word "God" appears almost as frequently in 1 Corinthians 1–4 as in all of the remaining twelve chapters.[2] The letter is addressed to "God's church as it is present in Corinth" (1.2), whose members are understood to be, collectively, "called" and "chosen" by God (1.2, 9, 24, 26, 27, 28), recipients of God's grace (1.4), and beneficiaries of God's faithfulness (1.9). They are subsequently described as God's "field" (3.9), God's "building" (3.9), and God's "temple" (3.16–17). In an important expository section, 1.18–2.16, Paul writes of the wisdom and saving power of God, and refers to his preach-

---

[1] The theological aspects of the argument in chapters 1–4 have been examined by, e.g., Peter Lampe, "Theological Wisdom and the 'Word About the Cross,'" *Interp* 44 (1990), 117–31; Thomas Söding, "Kreuzestheologie und Rechtfertigungslehre. Zur Verbindung von Christologie und Soteriologie im Ersten Korintherbrief und im Galaterbrief," *Catholica* 46 (1992), 31–60, esp. 36–45; Neil Richardson, *Paul's Language about God*, JSNTSup 99 (Sheffield, 1994), 95–138.

[2] In the Nestle-Aland edition of the Greek text (*Novum Testamentum Graece*, 27th edn. [Stuttgart, 1993]), *theos* occurs 49 times in chapters 1–4 (25 times just in the discourse on the wisdom of the cross, 1.18–2.16), and 54 times in chapters 5–16 (excluding two occurrences of the plural, "gods," in 8.5). Richardson, who has also noted this clustering, adds the observation that in many of its occurrences here, the word *theos* is particularly emphasized (*Paul's Language about God*, 107).

ing "the mystery of God" (2.1, NRSV).[3] Accordingly, he characterizes himself and other ministers not only as "servants of God"
(3.9) but also as "stewards of the mysteries of God" (4.1). Then in
drawing this first part of the letter to a close he refers to the power
of "God's reign" (4.20).

However, these chapters also make it clear that Paul believes his
stewardship of God's mysteries is fulfilled only as he proclaims the
cross, the gospel of Jesus Christ crucified (e.g., 1.17–18; 2.1–5).
Because his own life-changing experience of God's grace (15.8–10)
has left him in no doubt that knowing God involves belonging to
Christ, these two themes are closely interwoven in the fabric of his
thought. Moreover, what he means by knowing God overlaps with
what he means by believing in God (e.g., 1.21), and what he means
by belonging to Christ is hardly different from what he means by
being "in Christ" (e.g., 1.30; 3.1). Indeed, when we have come to
terms with what Paul is saying about knowing God and belonging
to Christ, we shall be very close to the theological center of 1
Corinthians, and with that, very close to the heart of his gospel as
it finds expression here. However, before turning to the principal
theological components of his argument in chapters 1–4, it is
important to take account of the specific practical issues that Paul
is addressing.

GOD'S CHURCH IN CORINTH

It is an open question how fully or precisely Paul himself understood the situation that obtained in his Corinthian congregation.
There is no way either to determine what he had learned about
developments since he had been in Corinth or to assess the accu-
racy of what he had learned. One can do no more than draw
certain inferences about his own perception of what was going on
there. This will provide at least some basis, however, for understanding why the appeals in 1.10–4.21 are formulated and supported as they are.

[3] Some ancient manuscripts have the word "testimony" (*martyrion*) instead of "mystery"
(*mystērion*) in 1 Cor. 2.1. Despite the arguments of Fee, *First Epistle*, 88, n. 1, the latter is to
be preferred; see Bruce M. Metzger, *A Textual Commentary on the Greek New Testament* (2nd
edn.; Stuttgart, 1994), 480, and Schrage, *Der erste Brief*, I.226.

A congregation at risk

As Paul understands it, his congregation is being torn apart by quarreling (1.11; 3.3), boasting (1.29; 3.21; 4.7), jealousy (3.3), and arrogance (4.6, 18, 19). He finds these manifested most clearly in the partisan heroizing of himself and Apollos (1.12; 3.4, 5–6, 21; 4.6) – and apparently also of Cephas (1.12), although it is highly unlikely that this Jerusalem apostle had ever been in Corinth. The boast of those who say, "I am Christ's" (1.12), is obviously of a different order. Perhaps they are claiming to have experienced some privileged revelation of Christ, and therefore to be independent of all human authorities. In any case, they come in for the same criticism as those who claim the privilege of association with Paul, Apollos, and Cephas.

Whatever the precise character of this partisanship, Paul seems also to have sensed that it was putting his own apostolic authority at risk. This is evident, for example, where he alludes to those who presume to pass judgment on him, when only the Lord can be his judge (4.3–5). It is also clear when he takes pains to point out that he alone is the "father" of the Corinthian church (4.15), and when he hints at the insubordination of some because they suppose he will not be returning (4.18). His appeal for unity in the congregation is therefore also an implicit appeal on behalf of his own authority over it.

The disruptions that the apostle sees in his congregation were probably the result of a competitive jockeying for status on the part of at least some and perhaps even many of its members. In Corinthian society, as in the Greco-Roman world generally, status was definitive for most aspects of a person's life. With status came honor, influence, and power. The possibility of advancing in status, thereby gaining further honor, influence, and power, depended in large measure on one's parentage, especially on whether one had been born slave or free. It also depended on the extent of one's wealth, one's success in garnering public honors, and whether one had well-placed friends.[4]

---

[4] See, e.g., Peter Garnsey, *Social Status and Legal Privilege in the Roman Empire* (Oxford, 1970); E. A. Judge, *Rank and Status in the World of the Caesars and St. Paul* (Christchurch, 1982); Clarke, *Secular and Christian Leadership in Corinth*, 23–39.

It was perhaps inevitable that this valuing of status and the symbols of status would be imported into the Corinthian church[5] and undergo in that setting a kind of sacralization. Within this religious community, people sought to advance their status not only with claims about belonging to this or that noted leader, but also with demonstrations of their own special religious wisdom and spiritual power. The apostle's concern about this situation is apparent when he remarks that there is no knowing God by means of worldly wisdom (1.21), and when he warns the Corinthians not to suppose that they are especially wise (3.18). It is evident, too, when he chides them about their pretentious claims already to be spiritually "enriched," as if to their own "honor" (1 Cor. 4.7, 8, 10; cf. 1.5, 7), and already to be spiritually empowered, as if they were even now participating in God's reign (4.8; cf. 4.19–20).

A congregation "called"

The argument in 1.10–4.21 is anchored at the beginning by an appeal for unity (1.10) and at the end by a summary appeal to become imitators of Paul (4.16). Almost at once, however, the first of these appeals gives way to an excursus on the strange "wisdom" of the cross (1.18–2.16), which provides its key theological foundation. Thus, as the call for unity is continued (3.1–4.13) the theme of the excursus is still present (3.18–23). The concluding, summary appeal to the Corinthians to become imitators of Paul is coupled with a reminder that he is, after all, their "father" in Christ (4.14–15); and it is followed by the warning that on his next visit he will have to chastise them, if in the meantime they do not change their ways (4.17–21).

The apostle is already beginning to lay the theological foundations for these appeals in the letter's prescript (1.1–3), where he gives more attention than usual to identifying those to whom he is writing (v. 2).[6] They are addressed not simply as a local religious society, but as a congregation that is representative of "God's

---

[5] Clarke, *Secular and Christian Leadership in Corinth*, esp. 89–107; cf. Meeks, *First Urban Christians*, 51–73.

[6] Contrast Rom. 1.1–7; 2 Cor. 1.1–2; Gal. 1.1–3; Phil. 1.1–2; 1 Thess. 1.1; Philem. 1.1–3 (cf. Eph. 1.1–2; Col. 1.1–2; 2 Thess. 1.1–2).

church" as a whole. They are also described as "sanctified in Christ Jesus" and "called to be holy people"; in Christ, and along with all who call him "Lord," they have been set apart for the service of God. The underlying conception here derives from Paul's Jewish heritage, and has particular affinities with Jewish apocalyptic texts which represent the elect of God as formed into an eschatological community of "holy people" (in some texts, simply "holy ones"), and called to remain faithful to God's covenant, even as God remains faithful to it.[7] From the outset, then, the Corinthians are being reminded that their true identity does not derive from their geographical location "in Corinth," or from their social location in Corinthian society (note 1.26). It derives, rather, from the holy God who has sanctified them – as Paul now believes – "in Christ Jesus," and formed them into a community of faith that embraces believers everywhere.

This understanding of the church as more inclusive than any local manifestation of it surfaces elsewhere in the letter, especially in 10.32 ("Give no offense . . . to the church of God" [NRSV]; cf. 11.22), 12.28 (there are diverse ministries "in the church"), and several places where Paul apparently has all of his own congregations in view (4.17; 7.17; 11.16; 14.33). The identification of God's church as a company of people who have been "called" also continues to be prominent in this letter, being carried forward, initially, into the thanksgiving (1.9), and then into the body of the letter (1.24, 26; 7.17–24). It expresses a sense both that believers now belong to the God by whom they have been formed into a believing community, and also that they no longer belong, in the same way as before, to the world in which God's call has come to them.

In particular, Paul wants the Corinthians to view themselves as a community called to holiness. This is not the only prescript in which he identifies the addressees as "holy people" (see 2 Cor. 1.1; Phil. 1.1), or even as "called to be holy people" (see Rom. 1.7). It is the only prescript, however, in which he describes them also as "sanctified [made holy] in Christ Jesus." The preposition in this phrase (Greek: *en*) is probably to be understood in a double sense,

---

[7] See Exod. 19.5–6; Lev. 22.32; Deut. 7.6; Tobit 8.15; *Pss. Sol.* 17.26–27; *1 Enoch* 62.7–8; 1QM iii.5; xii.7; 1QH vii.10; CD iv.6; and Schrage, *Der erste Brief*, I.103–104.

as signalling both the means and the sphere of sanctification.[8] Christ is the one *through* whom God's sanctifying action takes place and also the one *in* whom the believing community has its life as God's "holy people." This is another theme that Paul carries forward into the body of the letter. He reminds the Corinthians that Christ became sanctification for them (1.30); that their baptism marks them as members of a sanctified community (6.11), which is to be thought of as God's "holy temple" indwelt by the Spirit (3.16–17); and that their being God's "holy people" has important implications for their conduct both inside and outside the congregation (6.1, 2, 19; 7.34; cf. 14.33). Underlying all of these passages, and no less clear for being left unstated, is Paul's belief in the absolute holiness of God.

The theological foundations for Paul's subsequent appeals continue to be laid in the thanksgiving, 1.4–9. Like the prescript, it is unusual in the attention it gives to what identifies the addressees as a believing community. Paul's thanksgivings ordinarily include comments on his own present situation and on his past or anticipated relationships with those to whom he is writing.[9] In the present instance, however, the first person singular is present only in the opening formula of thanksgiving, and from that point forward everything centers on what distinguishes the letter's recipients as God's church.

Paul's primary expression of thanksgiving is for the grace of God that has been granted to the Corinthians in Christ Jesus (1.4–7a). What constitutes them as God's church is their life in Christ as beneficiaries of that grace. Although the apostle acknowledges the congregation's claim to have a complete inventory of spiritual gifts (vv. 5, 7a), it is evident that he regards these as deriving from and therefore incidental to their life in Christ, not definitive of it. Even as he is remarking on those gifts, he interjects the caveat that they flourish only to the extent that "the witness to Christ" (Paul's gospel) has been confirmed among them (1.6). The confirming of this witness takes place, as the rest of the letter will show, as believers allow their daily lives to be filled and shaped,

---

[8] Cf. Schrage, *Der erste Brief*, 1.103.

[9] See Rom. 1.8–15; 2 Cor. 1.3–7; Phil. 1.3–11; 1 Thess. I.2–10; Philem 4–7.

both corporately and individually, by the grace of God as they experience it in Christ. Having an abundance of spiritual gifts is therefore no cause for exulting in one's own status, only for giving thanks to God by whom they have been given (e.g., 4.7; chapters 12–14). Moreover, even the most impressive spiritual gifts have but temporary significance, because they belong only to this present, impermanent age (e.g., 8.2; 13.8–12).

In passing, yet not without reason, Paul accents the eschatological character of life in Christ by describing the Corinthians as awaiting "the day of our Lord Jesus Christ" that will bring his "revealing" from heaven (1.7b–8). It is clear from other parts of 1 Corinthians, notably chapter 15, that he thought this hope had been or was in danger of being given up by a fair number of people in his congregation. Thus here and elsewhere in the letter he leaves reminders for them that living from God's grace also means living in the sure hope of Christ's return and of God's final victory (see also 3.13–15; 4.4–5; 5.5; 11.26; 15.23, 24–28, 51–57). Meanwhile, and in preparation for Christ's return, the believing community continues to live from the strength that God provides.[10]

Paul's statement that "God is faithful" (v. 9a) echoes a traditional Jewish affirmation deeply rooted in Scripture.[11] Here it supports both his preceding comment about what believers will experience (v. 8) and his subsequent reference to what they have already experienced (v. 9b). Israel's confidence in God's faithfulness was integral to her sense of election and calling as God's covenant people, and was thus a fundamental component of the apostle's religious heritage.[12] However, there is nothing at all perfunctory about Paul's use of the traditional formula, either here or when he repeats it later in

---

[10] I interpret the relative pronoun that opens 1.8 (NRSV: "He") as referring to God, who is both the subject of the affirmation in v. 9 and the implied subject of the "divine passives" in vv. 4–6. But even if the antecedent of the pronoun is "our Lord Jesus Christ" (v. 7), God remains the ultimate source of the community's strengthening.

[11] See, e.g., Heb. 10.23; 11.11; 1 Pet. 4.19; 1 John 1.9; *1 Clem.* 27.1; *2 Clem.* 11.6, and the passages cited in n. 12.

[12] This finds expression in Deut. 7.9, "Know therefore that the Lord your God is God, the faithful God who maintains covenant loyalty with those who love him and keep his commandments, to a thousand generations" (NRSV). God was counted on to render just recompense for obedience and disobedience (Deut. 32.4; *Pss. Sol.* 17.10; *Pirke Aboth* 2.16), to keep every promise (Ps. 145.13 [LXX, 144.13]; Philo, *Allegorical Interpretation* 3.204; *The Sacrifices of Abel and Cain* 93; *Who Is the Heir of Divine Things?* 93; cf. *On the Change of Names* 182), and to give aid in times of distress (3 Macc. 2.11).

the letter (10.13; cf. 1 Thess. 5.24; 2 Cor. 1.18–20). For him, knowing God includes the experience of God's absolute dependability, and believing in God means trusting him wholly and unconditionally. In the context of this thanksgiving, the old affirmation expresses the apostle's specifically Christian understanding of God: that "the grace of God that has been given . . . in Christ Jesus" (1.4, NRSV) will be confirmed on the day of Christ's revealing (1.7b–8).

Further explication of God's grace and faithfulness is provided in the statement with which Paul concludes his thanksgiving, that by this absolutely dependable God the Corinthians "were called into the company [*koinōnia*] of his Son, Jesus Christ our Lord" (1.9b). It is not simply that God "invited" them to receive the gospel, but that they were actually transferred and transformed into the "company" of Christ.[13] The apostle understands God's call to be in itself an event of gracious, saving power; "those who are the called" (1.24, NRSV) are "those who are being saved" (1.18).

The association of God's grace and faithfulness with God's call is reminiscent especially of Second Isaiah (e.g., 41.9; 42.6; 48.12), but with the critical difference that Paul regards the elect community as distinguished by its life in Christ, not by its commitment to the law. For this reason, one might expect him to say that the Corinthians were called into a community of the "new covenant" established in Christ. This idea is not specifically present in 1 Corinthians, however, except perhaps indirectly when Paul cites the eucharistic saying, "This cup is the new covenant in my blood" (11.25, NRSV).[14] Instead, using a term that he could not have derived from the covenant language in his Greek Bible, he refers to the Corinthians as having been "called into the *koinōnia*" of God's Son. This Greek word suggests a more significant kind of relationship than its usual translation as "fellowship" is able to convey. It connotes "participation in," not just "association with." The apostle means that through God's saving call believers have come actually "to share in the life" (REB) that God has bestowed in Christ.

This sharing is twofold. Because they have been called to belong to Christ, which is the aspect of *koinōnia* that is foremost in

---

[13] Cf. Schrage, *Der erste Brief*, I.123.

[14] The clearest, but still only indirect evidence that Paul could think of the church as a new kind of covenant community comes from 2 Cor. 3.6 (cf. vv. 7–18) and Gal. 4.24–29.

1 Corinthians 1.9, believers have also been called into partnership with one another. They are joint shareholders – indeed, the term *koinōnia* was frequently used of business partnerships – in the life that God has given. These two aspects of being called into Christ's "company" are brought out clearly in chapter 10, where Paul refers to the community's sharing in the eucharistic cup and loaf as manifesting both its incorporation (*koinōnia*) into Christ (v. 16) and that "the many" are "one body" (v. 17).

This is the understanding of Christian community that underlies the appeal for unity in 1.10–17. Because, in response to God's call, the Corinthians were baptized into the name of Christ (not, e.g., into that of Paul), all of them (not just some) belong to Christ (not to a heroized leader of their own choosing); and since Christ is not "divided," they are to be one in him (1.12–13). The theological foundations of this appeal for unity had already been laid in the letter's prescript and thanksgiving, which manifest Paul's understanding of God as holy, gracious, and faithful, and that God's call is to be a holy people, "sanctified in Christ Jesus."

These theological foundations are still evident as the apostle resumes and concludes his appeal in 3.1–4.21. In a series of three metaphors he continues to urge the Corinthians to recognize that they are *God's* church, no one else's. They are God's "field" in which Paul and Apollos are only hired hands (3.6–9; cf. 4.1), God's "building" founded on Jesus Christ, to which many workers have contributed, all of them ultimately accountable to God (3.10–15), and more particularly, God's "temple," whose holiness must be kept inviolate (3.16–17).

Moreover, the apostle declares that in the end absolutely everyone and everything belongs to God, including – *at* "the end" – even Christ himself (3.21–23; cf. 15.24–28). He drives this point home to the Corinthians by asking them, rhetorically, "What do you have that you did not receive? And since you have received it, why do you boast as if you had not?" (4.7bc). If they are honest with themselves they will have to answer, "Nothing at all." Because everything belongs to God, they are in every respect beneficiaries of God's grace.

The eschatological orientation of Paul's thought also continues to be evident here. His argument presupposes a distinction between "this age" and an age that is yet to come (3.18), to which he refers – more often in 1 Corinthians than in the rest of his letters combined – as "God's reign" (4.20; see also 6.9, 10; 15.24, 50). It also presupposes that at the close of this present age the Lord will return (4.5; cf. 1.7b–8), and that when this "Day" of the Lord arrives people will be called to account for what they have done, and judged accordingly (3.8, 13–15, 17a; 4.4–5). This is why Paul mocks those in his congregation who claim to be experiencing "already" the full riches of salvation (4.8–10). As he sees it, whatever and however many the present gifts of God, those are not to be confused with the fullness, still to come, of "'what God has prepared for those who love him'" (2.11, NRSV).

For Paul, however, the present is not simply a time of waiting and preparing for the Lord's return. The argument in chapters 3 and 4 also continues to be shaped by his conviction that God's call has transferred believers even now into Christ's company, and has graced them even now with new life. His Corinthian hearers are already "in Christ," despite the fact that their understanding of what this means is still being formed (3.1; cf. 4.15, 17). Christ is already in place as the one and enduring "foundation" of their congregation (3.11), within which, in addition, God's Spirit is present (3.16). Because they now belong to Christ they can live with the confidence that they belong to God, and – at least in principle – no longer to this age, or even to death (3.21–23).

So far, we have seen that the apostle's appeal for congregational unity in chapters 1–4 is supported by theological foundations that are laid already in the letter's prescript and thanksgiving. His appeal is more directly supported, however, by the excursus in 1.18–2.16, which is one of the most important passages of sustained theological reflection in 1 Corinthians. This excursus not only provides the key theological component of the argument in chapters 1–4, it also sets the theological course of the letter as a whole. For these reasons, it deserves special attention.

THE WISDOM AND POWER OF GOD

The subject of Paul's excursus is the wisdom of the cross. This is most directly in view in 1.18–2.5, but it is still the underlying topic

in 2.6–16 (see 2.7, 8). According to Paul, it is the crucified Messiah
in whom the true character of God's wisdom is disclosed and
through whom God's saving power is at work. This theme, which
was perhaps anticipated in the rhetorical question of 1.13 ("Paul
wasn't crucified for you, was he?"), first surfaces in the transitional
remark of 1.17: Paul has been sent to proclaim the gospel, "yet not
in the wisdom that is grandly spoken, lest the cross be emptied of
its meaning."

God's wisdom and the world's

Paul offers, in the first place, a sharp-edged critique of what "this
age" ordinarily seeks and praises as wisdom (1.20). Specifically
religious wisdom is by no means exempt from his critique. Indeed,
his particular objective is to deflate the spiritual arrogance of those
in the Corinthian church who claim to be privileged with special
wisdom and knowledge about God, and therefore to be deserving
of special honors and status. No matter how religious its subject
matter, the wisdom they seek is strictly mundane (1.20; 2.6; 3.19)
and merely human (1.25; 2.5), and in their devotion to it they are
placing their trust ("exulting") in themselves rather than in the
Lord (1.29, 31; cf. 3.21; 4.7).

This critique of worldly wisdom does not amount to a condem-
nation of the world or of humanity as such. Later on, Paul will
affirm with the psalmist that "the earth and all that fills it" is God's
good creation (10.26, quoting Ps. 24.1). Rather, the target of his critique is humanity's attempt to know God through its own finite
wisdom, to take the measure of God by worldly calculations (1.21).
With this, God is reduced to an object of human conceiving, the
creature is confused with the Creator, and God's lordship over
creation is rejected in favor of creation's demands on God.[15] This
is the "wisdom," which is humanity's ultimate self-deception, that
Paul believes the cross unmasks as folly and brings to judgment
(3.18–20). It is, indeed, the folly of humanity's "sin" that he has in
view, although he does not use the word in this part of the letter.[16]

---

[15] Cf. Rom. 1.18–25, which, as often observed, reads almost like a commentary on 1 Cor. 1.21.

[16] There are only 11 occurrences of the word-group "sin" (*hamartia*, etc.) in the whole of 1
Corinthians (6.18*bis*; 7.28*bis*, 36; 8.12; 15.3, 17, 34, 56*bis*). The most theologically

Paul's choice of the *cross* (1.17, 18) and Jesus' *crucifixion* (1.23; 2.2, 8; cf. 1.13) to portray the content of his preaching is by no means incidental, either to the contrast that he is drawing between God's wisdom and the world's or to the rhetorical strategy that he is pursuing.[17] Even if the Corinthians are already familiar with his emphasis on the cross, as he claims (2.2), they could hardly fail to be surprised and disarmed by what they would certainly regard as inappropriate references to it in this context. In the religious groups to which most of them had once belonged, the cultic images were usually appealing symbols, within that culture, of fertility, life, and power – like a stalk of grain, a basket of fruit, or an erect phallus. But a cross, that infamous Roman instrument of execution, would be identified immediately by anyone in Roman Corinth with weakness, failure, shame, and death.[18]

Unless Galatians is earlier, 1 Corinthians is the first of the apostle's surviving letters in which this startling and powerful imagery appears. Because it is not found in any of the traditional statements about Jesus' death on which Paul has drawn (e.g., in 1 Cor. 5.7; 8.11; 11.23–26; 15.3), he may himself be the one who introduced it into the church's preaching. Whatever the case, in this excursus he is saying more than necessary about the cross if his point is only how Jesus was executed, and rather less than necessary about it if his point is only how much Jesus suffered. In this context his invoking of the cross is not primarily for either of these reasons, but in order to accentuate the radical disparity, even contradiction, that he sees between the wisdom of God and what passes for wisdom in this world.

---

significant of these are in a creedal formula about Christ's death "for our sins" (15.3; cf. vv. 17, 34), a summary statement about sin's relationship to the law and death (15.56), and Paul's warning that when one harms the conscience of a fellow believer one sins against Christ (8.12).

[17] Hans Dieter Betz, "The Problem of Rhetoric and Theology according to the Apostle Paul," in *L'Apôtre Paul: Personnalité, style et conception du ministère*, BETL 73 (ed. by A. Vanhoye; Leuven, 1986), 36–38, characterizes Paul's preaching of the cross as "direct display," a "rhetoric of demonstration" in distinction from the dialectical "rhetoric of persuasion," and refers especially to Gal. 3.1. Cf. Alexandra R. Brown, *The Cross and Human Transformation. Paul's Apocalyptic Word in 1 Corinthians* (Minneapolis, 1995).

[18] For discussions of crucifixion and attitudes toward it in the ancient world, see Martin Hengel, *Crucifixion in the Ancient World and the Folly of the Message of the Cross* (Philadelphia, 1977); Heinz-Wolfgang Kuhn, "Die Kreuzesstrafe während der frühen Kaiserzeit. Ihre Wirklichkeit und Wertung in der Umwelt des Christentums," *ANRW*, 2.25.1 (Berlin and New York, 1982), 648–793.

Paul does not mean simply that God is wiser or knows more than human beings.[19] More radically, he means that God's wisdom is of an entirely different order, "already decreed before the ages" (2.7; cf. Sir. 1.4; 24.9). Because it transcends the boundaries of time and space it remains in principle "secret and hidden" (2.7), quite beyond the reaches of any human inquiring or conceiving (2.9, 16).[20] This is why God's wisdom seems like foolishness when measured by worldly standards (1.25; cf. 1.18, 21, 27), and why the world's wisdom, when compared with God's, is exposed as actually foolish, even perverse. This is also why, to the extent that God's wisdom can be known at all, it has to be *revealed*. According to Paul, God has graciously done this through the agency of the Spirit (2.9–10), which all believers, not just the privileged, have received (2.12; cf. 12.12–13).[21] However, the actual place of this revealing remains the cross, where God's wisdom is both definitively present and powerfully active for salvation (1.18, 21–25; 2.2).

God's saving power

Throughout this excursus the apostle's critique of human wisdom is joined with affirmations about the saving power of God that is disclosed and operative in the cross. For Paul the word of the cross does not only indict the world for its folly, exposing humanity's bondage to sin. No less, it graces the world with life, bringing deliverance from sin's tyranny. Here the apocalyptic character of his thought is evident: even as the cross unmasks the folly of the world's wisdom, it establishes within this present age the power of the age to come. This is why he can say of the present, that "the

---

[19] As, e.g., in Sir. 15.18–19: "For great is the wisdom of the Lord; he is mighty in power and sees all things, his eyes are on those who fear him, and he has full knowledge of every human action." See also Sir. 42.18–21.

[20] The inaccessibility of God's wisdom was also sometimes a theme in the Jewish wisdom tradition; thus Sir. 24.28–29: "The first man did not know her [wisdom] fully, nor will the last one fathom her. For her thoughts are more abundant than the sea, and her counsel deeper than the great abyss" (NRSV); cf. Sir. 1.3.

[21] In the Jewish wisdom tradition, not the Spirit but the Torah is the medium of this revelation. While wisdom, like the law, can be called God's gift, it is also something that must be attained through disciplined study of the commandments and faithful obedience to them (e.g., Sir. 1.25–27; 4.11–19; 6.18–22, 37; 19.20; 24.23–24). There is, however, no evidence that the Christians of Corinth were associating wisdom and the law in this way.

ends of the ages have come" (10.11, NRSV), and of the word of the cross, that it is "the gospel" (1.17, 18) wherein the saving power of God is at work.[22]

Three important inferences may be drawn from the very first sentence of the excursus, where Paul has introduced a distinction between "those who are being saved" through the word of the cross and those who view the cross as foolishness and "are perishing" (1.18). From the outset, he is attributing salvation to the power of God that is operative in the cross, conceiving salvation as a relationship to God which enables human flourishing (life) as distinct from "perishing" (death), and thinking of salvation as an ongoing process, not yet completed. These are not points that Paul goes on to develop systematically, but they are implicit throughout the remainder of the letter.

First, the apostle regards salvation not only as God's doing but as proper to God's own being. In asserting that "God *decided*, through the foolishness of the kerygma, to save those who are believing" (1.21), he employs a verb (*eudokein*) that is often used in the Greek Old Testament with reference to the gracious favor and steadfast love that God is pleased to bestow on his people (e.g., Ps. 77[Greek, 76].7–9).[23] In the present context it suggests that providing for the salvation of humankind was God's free and deliberate act of grace.

For Paul, nothing comes closer to defining the reality of God than this will and power to save. The divine counsels about the salvation that God "has prepared for those who love him" (2.9, NRSV) lie hidden in "the very depths of God," so essential to who God is that they can be fathomed only by God's own Spirit (2.10–11b). This means that salvation is at God's initiative, not simply God's response to the importuning of a perishing humanity. Believers are "the called" of God (1.24, 26–29), recipients of what God has

---

[22] Contrast Karl Barth's contention that the one truly "positive" subject in 1 Corinthians is Christ's resurrection, because Paul regards that as the decisive event of God's saving power (*The Resurrection of the Dead* [London, 1933]). Everything before chapter 15, he believes, is "essentially critical and polemically negative" (107). For example, in the first four chapters Paul has set forth "the preaching of the Cross against the religious vivacity of the Corinthians in its remorseless negativeness as the insoluble paradox, as the angel with the flaming sword in front of the shut gates of Paradise" (23).

[23] See, esp., Ceslaus Spicq, *Theological Lexicon of the New Testament* (Peabody, 1994), II.99–103.

chosen to reveal (2.9–10), beneficiaries of the gifts that God has chosen to bestow (2.12). It is in the cross, according to Paul, that one can see God taking the initiative. There the eschatological wisdom and power of God have penetrated into this present age, unmasking its ersatz wisdom and power, and calling an alienated humanity to receive the gift of life (1.26–31). He therefore proclaims "Jesus Christ, and him crucified" as the one in whom the reality of God is definitively revealed, and in whom the power of the coming age is already decisively at work for salvation (1.23–24, 30; 2.2, 4–5).

Second, Paul associates humanity's flourishing with its coming truly to "know God." This is what the world has failed to attain through its own wisdom, and what God has made possible through the wise foolishness of the cross for "those who are believing" (1.21). Here, as throughout the letter, it is evident that the apostle conceives of knowing God as inseparable from belonging to the crucified Christ. It is also evident that by knowing God he means more than having some knowledge *about* God and God's "secret purposes" (as, e.g., in Wisd. 2.21–24). It involves "believing" in God, and is the *relationship* to God which he describes as trusting ("exulting") in the Lord rather than self as the source of life and its flourishing (1.29, 31). Being saved therefore means being delivered from the self-deception that is intrinsic to worldly wisdom, and that diminishes humanity by alienating it, in its folly, from God.

What the apostle means by this coming to know God, which he associates with "being saved," is further clarified in 1.26–31. Here he asks the Corinthians to understand their own conversion to the gospel as a demonstration of the saving power of the cross. In part, he is drawing their attention to the *circumstances* in which they had been "called into the company of [God's] Son" (1.9). Only a few of them enjoyed the privileged status that society accords those who, by the world's standards, are wise, powerful, and well-born (1.26). Nevertheless, as Paul says several times over, God *called* and *chose* them for something better (1.26, 27, 28). Here he is drawing from the scriptural stock of terms for divine election, and thereby emphasizing yet again the priority of God's saving grace.[24]

---

[24] See, e.g., Deut. 4.37; 7.7; 10.15; 14.2; 1 Kgs. 3.8; Pss. 33.12; 78.68; 135.4; Isa. 41.8–9; 43.10; 44.1–2.

Especially, Paul wants the Corinthians to recognize that there is a particular reason why God's call came to them, people who had no particular standing in the eyes of the world. He cannot and does not claim that it was to reverse or even improve their worldly fortunes. As he writes, most of them are still "nobodies" in Corinth. Rather, he suggests that God's purpose in calling them was to expose as shameful and self-defeating what the world commonly esteems as honorable and ennobling (1.27–28). Beyond this, they are to understand that God's purpose was to call them to the true source of their life, which is "in Christ Jesus" (1.30). Here, as throughout the excursus, Paul means the *crucified* Christ who is "God's wisdom and God's power" (1.24). Because they are in Christ, their relationship to the world has changed even if their circumstances in the world have not. Although they remain in this present, passing age, it can no longer claim them as its own. Their identity is now established in their belonging to Christ, their lives are now marked by the sign of his cross.

Paul formulates his statement about the Corinthians' new status very emphatically: "*You are* in Christ Jesus." Their life in Christ is a present and corporate, as well as individual, reality. He also formulates his statement quite deliberately, taking care to say that Christ "*became for us* wisdom from God, as well as righteousness, sanctification, and redemption." He does not say that Christ has bestowed these on believers. The Corinthians are therefore wrong to suppose that God's wisdom, for example, is to any degree at their disposal or can belong to them. Rather, it is a matter of *their* belonging to the crucified Christ, in whose company they are enlivened and sustained by God's own wisdom, and by the righteousness, sanctification, and redemption that are given in Christ.[25]

The apostle seems to take it for granted that his congregation is familiar with these last three terms, because he offers no exposition of them. The word "righteousness" occurs only here in 1 Corinthians, although the related verb ("to rectify") appears in a statement about the Corinthians' baptism: "You were washed, . . . you were sanctified, . . . you were rectified" (6.11). Whether we may

---

[25] Cf. Schrage, *Der erste Brief*, I.188, 215; Walter Klaiber, "Rechtfertigung und Kreuzesgeschehen," *Das Wort vom Kreuz: Geschehen – Denken – Theologie* (ed. by Erich Lubahn and Otto Rodenberg; Giessen and Basle, 1988), 95.

presume for this letter the full Pauline meaning of righteousness, as developed especially in Galatians and Romans, is uncertain. It is clear, however, that Paul is associating righteousness, as he has baptism itself (1.13), with the life that derives from belonging to the crucified Christ.

The reference here to "sanctification" corresponds to the pre-script, where Paul has addressed the Corinthians as "sanctified in Christ Jesus, called to be holy people" (1.2; cf. 6.11). For Israel, the sanctifying event was her deliverance from Egypt, which she experienced both as liberation from oppression and as God's forming her into a holy people, called and set apart ("consecrated") for obedience to the law (e.g., Lev. 11.44–45; 20.7–8, 24–26; 22.32–33; Num. 15.40–41). Paul, following the church's tradition, identifies sanctification with Christ, and – perhaps going beyond the church's tradition – thinks specifically of his crucifixion as the sanctifying event. For Paul, it is therefore the cross (not the law, as for the Jews) that establishes and nourishes the identity of this believing community. But still, for him, to be sanctified as God's people is to be consecrated to the service of God.

The idea of "redemption," like that of sanctification, was deeply rooted in the church's Scripture, where it describes both Israel's deliverance from Egypt (e.g., Exod. 6.6; Deut. 7.8; 9.26; Ps. 77.15) and her return from exile (e.g., Isa. 43.1, 14; 44.22–24). Paul uses the term itself only in this one statement in 1 Corinthians and in two passages in Romans (3.24; 8.23).[26] From the present context, and more directly from his use of a traditional formulation in Romans 3.24–25, it is apparent that he, like the church's traditions, identifies Christ's death as decisive for the redemption of humankind.[27] Perhaps surprisingly, given the theme of this excursus, Paul seems not to be thinking specifically of humanity's liberation from its bondage to worldly wisdom. All three traditional terms are used here rather generally, to emphasize that those who belong to Christ have come to know the God in whom they have life.[28]

---

[26] It is somewhat more prominent in the disputed Paulines, occurring in Eph. 1.7, 14; 4.30; Col. 1.14; cf. Titus 2.14.

[27] This tradition is also present, e.g., in Eph. 1.7 and Heb. 9.15; cf. Mark 10.45; Titus 2.14; 1 Pet. 1.18–19.

[28] Even if his later references to the Corinthians as having been "bought and paid for" (6.20; 7.23) imply some notion of Christ's death as a "ransom," which is questionable,

Knowing God continues to be a theme in the second part of the excursus (2.6–16), where Paul writes of the Spirit's presence among those who are being saved and of how this distinguishes them from those who are perishing. However, he does not view the Spirit as the source of salvation, or the Spirit-filled community (or individuals) as the locus of God's saving power, as some in Corinth apparently did. He identifies the Spirit's role as mediating the knowledge of God that is revealed in the word of the cross (2.10–15). For Paul, the wisdom of the cross cannot be perceived apart from the work of the Spirit; but equally, the work of the Spirit does not take place in isolation from the power of the cross.[29]

Given that Paul's attention has been focused since 1.18 on the wisdom of the cross, when he concludes his excursus by asserting that believers "have the mind of Christ" (2.16b) he must surely mean the mind of the *crucified* Christ. This statement qualifies, without actually setting aside, the negative answer that is presupposed by the rhetorical question he has just quoted from Isa. 40.13 (Greek version): "Who has known the mind of the Lord, to be able to instruct him?" (2.16a). From the apostle's standpoint, in so far as the counsels of God can be known in this age they have been disclosed in "Jesus Christ, and him crucified." In the apparent folly and weakness of the cross, those who have received the Spirit from God not only discern but experience the gracious, saving power of God that constitutes the reality of God – God's being *for* them (cf. Rom. 8.31–32), devoted to their flourishing.

Moreover, since those who are being saved from perishing have been formed into a community that lives from the cross, they are also summoned to be informed, both individually and corporately, by the mind of the crucified Christ. Throughout most of the rest of the letter the apostle is instructing his congregation on how this norm is

---

this facet of the metaphor remains completely undeveloped. In the civil sphere, certainly, "redemption" meant the securing of freedom through payment of a ransom, as for prisoners of war. In the case of Israel's redemption, however, the point is not that ransom has been paid (note Isa. 52.3, "you shall be redeemed without money"), but that God can be trusted to deliver his people from oppression. See Karl Kertelge, "ἀπολύτρωσις," *EDNT*, I.138–40; Schrage, *Der erste Brief*, 1.216.

[29] Contrast the comments of Gordon Fee, *God's Empowering Presence*, 93–110, who finds Paul in this passage (and overall) assigning a significantly more fundamental role to the Spirit than I am suggesting here.

to guide them in dealing with the particularities of their own situation, as God's church in Corinth. But his most fundamental point is already evident: in disclosing God's will and power to save, that God cares and provides for humanity's flourishing, the word of the cross is a word of grace. Therefore, the community that lives from the cross lives from grace, and informed by the mind of Christ devotes itself as God is devoted to the flourishing of all creation.

The third point signaled in the opening sentence of the excursus is that the knowledge of God's wisdom and power revealed in the cross, and the trustful believing in God that characterizes those who are in Christ, do not in themselves constitute salvation. Paul refers to believers as those who are "being saved," not as those who have come into the fullness of salvation. Indeed, the noun "salvation" (*sōtēria*) does not appear even once in 1 Corinthians. Only verbal forms are used, and always with reference either to the present working of God's saving power or to its fulfillment in the future.[30] In the latter cases, the future in view is not some later point in this present age (1.20, 21, 27, 28; 2.6, 8, 12), which Paul describes as in the process of passing away (7.31), but "God's reign" (e.g., 4.20), which will come at "the end" (15.24, 50). For him, the life in Christ with which believers are graced is no less real for their having received it in this present, passing age; but the consummation of salvation is a knowledge of God that will be granted only in God's own future. Until then, the sign of the saving power of God from which the believing community draws its life is not the victor's crown, as the Corinthians seem to believe. For Paul, God's final victory is yet to be given, the "imperishable wreath" is yet to be conferred (15.54–57; 9.25). In this age, and for however long it may continue, God's saving power is present in the cross of Christ. The Corinthians are therefore called to live under the sign of this cross and in conformity with what it discloses about true power and wisdom.

BELONGING TO CHRIST, BELONGING TO GOD

Paul's distinction between the world's wisdom and God's is recapitulated and applied in the summary appeals and assertions of

---

[30] See 1.18, 21; 3.15; 5.5; 7.16; 9.22; 10.33; 15.2.

3.18–23 where he is reinforcing his call for unity in the congregation. These few verses thus provide a focused view of the theological orientation of chapters 1–4. In doing so, they also help to confirm the observation with which our examination of these chapters began, that what Paul says about knowing God is not to be separated from what he says about belonging to Christ, and that these twin themes take us very close to the heart of his gospel as it is found in this letter.

Paul wants the Corinthians to understand that those who trust in the wisdom of this age and heroize human leaders do not flourish, but are to be counted among the perishing. By thus yielding to the tyrannical powers of this age (cf. 2.6) they are turning away from God, thereby alienating themselves from the source of their life. When he directs them to become "fools" that they may become "wise" (3.18; cf. 4.10a) he is directing them to the wisdom of the cross, rejected by this age (cf. 2.8) but the means by which God has unmasked humanity's folly (3.20, citing Ps. 94.11; cf. 1.19, citing Isa. 29.14) and provided for its salvation (1.21–25). He is urging them to reappropriate the gospel through which God called them to be baptized into the company of Christ (1.9), and with that into the believing community of "those who are being saved" (cf. 1.18–21).

The fundamental warrant for this appeal is provided by the closing affirmations of the paragraph (3.21b–23). These have a rhetorical power that is appropriate to their exceptional theological significance: "For everything belongs to you – whether Paul or Apollos or Cephas, or the world, or life or death, or present or future – everything belongs to you, and you belong to Christ, and Christ belongs to God." As believers, the Corinthians are no longer beholden to the world (*kosmos*) or anything in it, not even to those who have established and nurtured them in the gospel. Rather, the whole created order, in both its spatial and temporal dimensions, belongs to them – although not, of course, in the same way that it belongs to God (e.g., 10.26). It "belongs" to them in the sense that they have been delivered from all the threats and terrors of this age, including even the terror of death, that would otherwise exercise control over them. This deliverance does not consist in their own empowerment, as if they could hope to defeat the forces that would diminish and destroy their lives. It consists in *their* belonging to Christ, and through him to God, even as Christ himself belongs to God. Paul means their belonging to "Jesus Christ, and him crucified," in whom they have come to know God. In this knowing they are enabled to receive their lives as graced and claimed by the saving power of God's love, and also – even in this present age – to live with a sure hope that God's saving power will prevail. This ultimate victory of God is the apostle's subject in chapter 15, where a snapshot of "the end" when God will be "all in all" (15.24–28) suggests why he can refer even to Christ as belonging to God.

CHAPTER 3

Belonging to Christ in an unbelieving society

The apostle's call for unity in the congregation (chapters 1–4) has been at the same time a call to reaffirm and realize the consequences of the new self-understanding that is given with life in Christ. Paul's hearers are to understand themselves as "God's church in Corinth," called by the holy, gracious, and faithful God whose wisdom and saving power have been disclosed in "Jesus Christ, and him crucified." Both individually and corporately they belong to Christ and therefore to God (3.21–23).

Throughout the first four chapters, but especially in the excursus of 1.18–2.16, Paul has been distinguishing at least implicitly between "this age" (or "the world") and an age that is yet to come.[1] Although the coming age, which is "God's reign" (4.20), has been inaugurated in the cross where God's saving power is already at work, the Corinthians would be quite wrong to regard it as somehow fulfilled already (4.8). This "already but not yet" of life in Christ means that the believers in Corinth must reckon for the time being with a dual identity. Fundamentally, in their belonging to Christ and to God they belong to God's reign. Thus, as *God's church* they comprise an eschatological community, a community of the end-time. However, as God's church *in Corinth* they also comprise a "present-time" community with a specific social location and continuing social identity.

To the extent that Paul's congregation was noticed at all by the wider Corinthian public, it was likely regarded as simply another of the city's offbeat religious societies with roots in distant parts of the Mediterranean world. Perhaps many would have been unable

---

[1] See 1.20, 21, 27; 2.6, 8, 12; 3.18, 19, 22; 4.9, 13.

to distinguish the members of this religious society from Jews,
whom they also knew to believe in only one God, beside whom
there can be no other. The Jews themselves, of course, would have
rejected as blasphemous the church's claims about Jesus, and
would have regarded its interpretations of their scriptures as down-
right perverse. Inevitably, then, to the extent that Paul's Corinthian
converts were taking seriously their new identity as "God's
church," their continuing social identity as ordinary Corinthians
was being rendered problematic. How could they be God's church
in Corinth?

This is the situation that the apostle has in view in 5.1–11.1, the
next major section of his letter. Here, too, believers are understood to constitute a community of the end-time ("on whom the
ends of the ages have come," 10.11 [NRSV]), situated in but not
finally belonging to a world that will not endure (7.29–31; cf. 5.10;
6.2–3; 7.33, 34). The issues that Paul is addressing in these chapters all reflect the difficulty of belonging to Christ in an unbelieving society. His responses to these issues are based on the
theological foundations that he has already laid in the letter's prescript and thanksgiving, especially in his excursus on the wisdom
of the cross. This is evident when he refers or alludes to
Christ's death, even though without mention of "the cross" or
"crucifixion" (e.g., 5.7b; 8.11). It is equally clear when, in various
ways, he reminds the Corinthians that their true identity inheres
in their belonging to Christ, and through Christ to God (e.g.,
6.12–20; 8.1–6).

OBSERVING BOUNDARIES

Broadly considered, chapters 5–7 are devoted to problems that fall
under the general category of sexual immorality (*porneia*),[2]
although this statement has to be qualified in two respects. First, it
is unclear whether, and if so, how, the counsels about taking fellow
believers to court (6.1–11) are related to the matter of sexual immorality. Second, in chapter 7 the apostle's concerns about sexual

---

[2] Terms from this word-group appear in all three chapters: 5.1, 9, 10, 11; 6.9, 13, 15, 16, 18;
7.2. Elsewhere in 1 Corinthians they occur only in 10.8, and elsewhere in the undisputed
Paulines only in Rom. 1.29; 2 Cor. 12.21; Gal. 5.19; 1 Thess. 4.3.

immorality are expressed only as he responds to the more fundamental question, whether for believers sexual relationships are ever
moral, even within marriage. The theological foundations of his
counsels in these three chapters are most evident in 6.12–20,
7.17–24, and 7.29–35.

The issue in 8.1–11.1 is whether it is appropriate for believers to
partake of meat from animals that have been slaughtered in connection with pagan sacrificial rites. Does eating meat left over
from pagan sacrifices make one an idolater? Paul supports his
counsels about this mainly by drawing an analogy between what
he is recommending to the Corinthians and his own practice of
declining to exercise certain rights in order to win more people to
the gospel (chapter 9). However, underlying this appeal to his personal example (see also 8.13; 10.32–11.1) are his views about
knowing God and belonging to Christ. These surface when he is
introducing the topic (8.1–6), at certain special points as he proceeds with his discussion of it (e.g., 8.11; 9.21; 10.26), in his
warning about idolatry (10.1–22), and as he brings his counsels to
a close (10.31).

It is not surprising to find the topics of sexual immorality and
idolatry juxtaposed, as they are in this part of the letter. In
Jewish traditions sexual immorality is often mentioned along
with idolatry, and one is typically identified as representative of
the other (see, especially, Wisd. 14.12, 22–29; also *Sib. Or.* 3.8–45;
T. Reu. 4.6; *T. Sim.* 5.3; *T. Naph.* 3.4). Here, Paul himself quite
specifically connects them when he draws on Israel's experience
in the wilderness to warn his congregation about both evils
(10.7–8). For the apostle as for the Jews, rejecting idolatry and
abstaining from the sexual immorality that goes with it are key
identity markers of the faithful community. The question that
the Corinthians are facing, and now Paul along with them, is
exactly what constitutes transgression of the boundaries, thus
marked, by which God's church is to maintain its distinctiveness
within pagan society.[3]

Paul's concern that his congregation observe the appropriate

---

[3] For a discussion of the importance of community boundaries with special reference to
the Pauline congregations, see Meeks, *First Urban Christians*, 84–107.

boundaries is evident throughout these chapters.[4] For example, he believes that the church member who has been cohabiting with his stepmother[5] has drifted over a boundary into pagan territory (5.1), and that he should now be numbered among the "outsiders" (5.12–13). He also believes that a line has been crossed whenever disputes between church members are taken to pagan magistrates for arbitration, which involves "the unrighteous" sitting in judgment over "the saints" (6.1–6, 9–11). Again, when Paul warns about sexual immorality (6.12–20) he is thinking of a boundary separating those who belong to Christ from those who do not (e.g., vv. 15a, 17). Following this, in chapter 7, he distinguishes (implicitly) between marrying "in the Lord" (v. 39), meaning within the Christian community, and marrying an outsider. Finally, his appeals on behalf of "the weak" (8.1–11.1) are no less appeals that others not encourage them, however inadvertently, to wander back across the boundary line that separates (Gentile) believers from their former idolatry.

These chapters make it equally clear, however, that Paul knows it is not easy for the community to maintain a sense of its distinctive identity, and to be faithful in observing the boundaries deemed to be appropriate to that identity. He is quite aware that neither the community as such nor its individual members can remain completely detached from the world (5.10). Believers necessarily have various dealings with the social, political, and economic institutions of this passing age (7.29–32; cf. 10.25), probably many of them

---

[4] Pertinent studies that also take account of this concern include: Peder Borgen, " 'Yes,' 'No,' 'How Far?': The Participation of Jews and Christians in Pagan Cults," *Paul in His Hellenistic Context* (ed. by T. Engberg-Pedersen; Minneapolis, 1995), 256–90; L. William Countryman, *Dirt, Greed, and Sex. Sexual Ethics in the New Testament and Their Implications for Today* (Philadelphia, 1988), 190–214; Benjamin Fiore, "Passion in Paul and Plutarch: 1 Corinthians 5–6 and the Polemic against Epicureans," *Greeks, Romans, and Christians. Essays in Honor of Abraham J. Malherbe* (ed. by D. L. Balch, E. Ferguson, and W. A. Meeks; Minneapolis, 1990), 135–43; Wayne A. Meeks, "The Polyphonic Ethics of the Apostle Paul," *The Annual of the Society of Christian Ethics* (Knoxville, TN, 1988), 17–29; Alan C. Mitchell, "Rich and Poor in the Courts of Corinth: Litigiousness and Status in 1 Corinthians 6.1–11," *NTS* 39 (1993), 562–86; James T. South, "A Critique of the 'Curse/Death' Interpretation of 1 Corinthians 5.1–8," *NTS* 39 (1993), 539–61; Martin, *Corinthian Body*.

[5] So most interpreters, although the woman involved may well have been the (deceased) father's concubine (thus Craig Steven De Vos, "Stepmothers, Concubines and the Case of Πορνεία in 1 Corinthians 5," *NTS* 44 (1998), 104–14).

as slaves of unbelieving masters (7.21), and perhaps a few as masters of unbelieving slaves (7.22). Some have unbelieving spouses (7.12–15), others may be betrothed to unbelievers (cf. 7.39). Doubtless all have other kinfolk, various associates, and countless acquaintances who are outsiders.

In addition, the apostle himself allows for certain crossings of the boundaries, and in both directions. He regards his own principal work as persuading unbelievers to cross over into faith (9.19–23). He conceives of the possibility that on occasion an unbelieving husband or wife may be won over by the believing spouse (7.16). He seems to be quite at ease with the fact that outsiders sometimes cross a boundary to visit in the Christian assembly (14.23–25). Indeed, Paul does not rule out in principle that believers may occasionally cross in the other direction to dine in a pagan temple (8.10),[6] and he simply takes it as a matter of course that believers will sometimes gladly accept dinner invitations from unbelievers (10.27). However, there are also instances, as in the case of the man who has been living with his father's wife, when he thinks it necessary that an insider be regarded once more as an outsider, and therefore separated from the faithful community (5.12–13). It is possible that Paul is allowing for this man's repentance and eventual restoration, as in the case on which he offers counsel in 2 Corinthians 5.1–11.[7] If so, that would mean the man's crossing over the boundary yet again, becoming an "insider" once more. In all of these instances, a certain blurring of the boundaries between the church and its social environment is taking place, even as the importance of observing those boundaries is being affirmed.

Paul's remarks in 6.1–11 point to another sense in which boundaries can be blurred. His initial counsel (vv. 1–6) is that "the saints" should not be taking their legal disputes before pagan magistrates, who are of "the unrighteous" (*hoi adikoi*). His greater

---

[6] Borgen, "'Yes,' 'No,'" 55–56.

[7] South, "A Critique of the 'Curse/Death' Interpretation," shows that Paul's directive in 1 Corinthians 5 could well have in view the eventual restoration of the incestuous man's "insider" status. In 2 Cor. 2.5–11, which is certainly dealing with a different case (Furnish, *II Corinthians*, 160–68), Paul specifically appeals for the restoration of a member who has been disciplined by exclusion.

concern, however, is that wrongdoing (*adikein*) is present at all within the church, and along with it the corresponding impulse to seek legal remedies (vv. 7–8). In these respects believers are already beginning to resemble unbelievers, even if in other ways the boundaries between the church and the world appear to remain intact.[8]

The counsels about marriage (chapter 7) and eating meat from pagan temples (8.1–11.1) disclose a related problem. Some boundary lines cannot be exactly drawn or firmly fixed.[9] Sexual relationships apart from marriage are clearly out of bounds for those who are in Christ (e.g., 6.12–20). But what of marriage itself? Sometimes yes and sometimes no. Paul draws the line in different places, depending on the specific circumstances (7.8–9, 25–28, 32–38). Even in the matter of divorce, which he normally considers out of bounds (7.10, 11b), circumstances may require a redrawing of the line (7.15; cf. 7.11a). Idolatry, of course, is always out of bounds (e.g., 10.21). But where exactly is the line to be drawn between innocent partaking of meat, even in a temple dining room, that has been left over from pagan sacrifices, and involving oneself in an act of pagan worship? In fact, as in the cases of marriage and divorce, precisely where the line is to be located will depend on the particular situation (8.1–10; 10.25–27; 10.28).

HOLDING TO THE CENTER

If the realities of everyday life often render the boundaries between the church and the world indistinct and shifting, this only accentuates the fact that these boundaries, no matter how well they may mark and maintain the community's identity, are not actually definitive of it. As Paul sees it, the community's identity is given in and with the gospel, through which believers have been called of God into Christ's company. For the apostle, belonging to Christ is not mainly about drawing boundaries and keeping them inviolate, but about holding fast to the gospel (10.12; 15.1–2). The gospel is the vital center to which the boundaries themselves must be oriented, and in accord with which they must be plotted, monitored,

---

8   Cf. Mitchell, "Rich and Poor in the Courts of Corinth," 565–66, commenting on the parallelism of 6.6, 8.

9   Cf. Borgen's comment about the matter of idolatry, "'Yes,' 'No,'" 47.

and redrawn when necessary. Moreover, Paul is confident that this same gospel that makes certain boundaries imperative in the present age will, in the age to come, render all such boundaries obsolete. After all, what drives and shapes his mission to "outsiders" is the conviction that no one stands beyond the circle of God's saving purpose, and that, in this sense, even unbelievers are "insiders" to God's grace (see 9.19–23).

There is no theological excursus in 5.1–11.1 that is comparable, at least in length, with the discourse on the wisdom of the cross in 1.18–2.16. However, throughout these chapters the apostle supports his counsels and directives with affirmations about the gospel, thereby reminding his hearers that they have been graced with new life and claimed for Christ. For example, and in keeping with the theological foundations laid in earlier chapters, he reminds them that they live from Christ's death (5.7b–8; 8.11; cf. 1.18–2.16), that they have been rectified and sanctified in him (6.11; cf. 1.2, 30), and that they, along with all who belong to Christ's company (*koinōnia*), have been incorporated into one body (10.16–17; cf. 1.9). There are four passages in particular where Paul makes comments that can further our understanding of the theological point of view from which he is writing, both in this section and in the letter overall.

Belonging to another

The subject of 6.12–20 is indicated by the summary appeal in v. 18a, "Distance yourselves from *porneia*." In this directive the word *porneia* can refer either to going to prostitutes or, inclusively, to all sexual relationships that are regarded as immoral. If Paul means the latter, as seems likely, he is thinking not only of a man's "having sex" with a female prostitute (*pornē*, vv. 15b, 16a), but also of incestuous relationships like the one about which he has just written (chapter 5), the sexual offenses mentioned in the vice list of 6.9–10, and, indeed, any sexual relationship that is not between the partners in a marriage (7.2; cf. 6.9).[10]

No specific instance of sexual immorality is addressed in

---

[10] In the following I am indebted at a number of points to Renate Kirchhoff's informative study, *Die Sünde gegen den eigenen Leib: Studien zu πόρνη und πορνεία in 1 Kor 6,12–20 und dem sozio-kulturellen Kontext der paulinischen Adressaten*, SUNT 18 (Göttingen, 1994).

6.12–20, although it is possible that Paul means to be supplementing and supporting his instructions about how to deal with the
incestuous man (chapter 5). Alternatively, or in addition, these
comments could be read in connection with chapter 7, where he
replies to a number of questions about sex and marriage which
have been put to him in a letter from his congregation. In any
event, he introduces his topic with a slogan, "Everything is permissible for me" (v. 12), which he qualifies in two ways even as he gives
it: "but not everything is beneficial . . . [and] I will not permit
myself to be dominated by anything." The slogan, which appears
again in 10.23, may have originated in Corinth or it could be Paul's
own formulation. Whichever the case, by simultaneously introducing and qualifying it the apostle is preparing his hearers for the
point that he goes on to make in vv. 13–19: for those who are in
Christ, *porneia* is never permissible.[11]

Paul bases his case against *porneia* on the premise, for which he
is probably dependent on the church's tradition, that "God raised
the Lord and will raise us, too, by his power" (v. 14; cf. 2 Cor. 4.14;
Rom. 8.11). This is the first and only mention of Christ's resurrection in 1 Corinthians until chapter 15, where the point expressed
here underlies the entire argument. The resurrection of Christ has
been presupposed, of course, all along. For Paul, the saving power
of God that is evident in the cross (1.18, 24; 2.4, 5) is identical with
the power that raised Jesus from the dead, and that will be fully
established in the coming reign of God (4.20; 15.24–28, cf. v. 43).
Thus for Paul, the crucified Christ is identical with the resurrected
Lord.[12]

In the present context, Paul's statement that "God . . . will raise
us, too" supports his claim that "the body is not for sexual immorality but for the Lord, and the Lord for the body" (v. 13b). Here as
elsewhere he means much more by "body" (*to sōma*) than just the
physical body that one "has." He is thinking of the whole person,
a "self" which, precisely in its corporeality and creatureliness, is
capable of communicating with and therefore relating to other
selves. However, what he sees as finally definitive of one's humanity is the body's being "for the Lord" and the Lord's being "for the

---

[11] Cf. ibid., e.g., 75–84.   [12] Below, 117–20.

body." He thus regards the body as the place where the claim of the resurrected-crucified Lord is received, and where his lordship is to be manifested.[13] Moreover, he understands the lives of those who accept Christ's lordship as significantly qualified, both by the assurance of their own ultimate resurrection with him (v. 14) and by the reigning presence with them of God's Spirit (v. 19a). Paul's comment about the relationship between the body and the Lord therefore particularizes for the present context his earlier and more general affirmation that believers belong to Christ, and through Christ, to God (3.21–23). In this relationship, founded on God's gracious call, they are wholly claimed for the service of God and thereby freed from the tyranny of all competing claims.

The apostle's premise about the relationship between the body and the Lord underlies several other affirmations in 6.12–20: "your bodies are members of Christ" (v. 15a); "your body is a temple of the indwelling Holy Spirit, which you have from God, and you are not your own" (v. 19); "you were bought and paid for" (v. 20a). Along with the basic premise on which they rest, these statements provide the context within which Paul's two qualifications of the introductory slogan (v. 12) are to be understood. Whatever actions respect and reflect the believer's relationship to the Lord are "beneficial," and therefore permissible. Whatever actions threaten to exercise their own control over the believer's life are thereby subversive of this relationship, and therefore not permissible.

Several further points merit special attention. One of these is the parallel that Paul draws between the body's relationship to the Lord (v. 13b) and the relationship of food to the stomach (v. 13a). Some interpreters have argued that part or all of the remark about food and the stomach is a Corinthian slogan, which either has been

---

[13] For Paul's understanding of *sōma* see, esp., Ernst Käsemann, *Leib und Leib Christi: Eine Untersuchung zur paulinischen Begrifflichkeit*, BHT 9 (Tübingen, 1933), e.g., 119–25; idem, "1. Korinther 6,19–20," *Exegetische Versuche und Besinnungen 1* (Göttingen, 1960), 276–79; idem, "The Pauline Doctrine of the Lord's Supper," *Essays on New Testament Themes*, SBT 41 (Naperville, 1964), 108–35, 129–30, 132–33; idem, "On Paul's Anthropology," *Perspectives on Paul* (Philadelphia, 1971), 1–31; idem, "The Theological Problem Presented by the Motif of the Body of Christ," ibid., 102–21, 114–16. Käsemann's views have also informed the discussions by Kirchhoff, *Die Sünde*, 130–45, and Schrage, *Der erste Brief*, II.21–30, 33–34, etc. Martin, approaching the subject by way of Greco-Roman medical and philosophical conceptions of the body (*Corinthian Body*), makes no reference to Käsemann's work.

or could be applied to justify a certain moral indifferentism about sexual relationships.[14] However, Paul's rhetoric here is not polemical but didactic, and there is no difficulty in regarding the whole of v. 13 as his own thought. Renate Kirchhoff has shown that his argument is in certain respects similar to one in the Jewish *Testament of Naphtali* (2.2–10; 3.2–4), which calls for obedience to the law by associating the moral order that God commands with the physical order that God established at creation.[15] It follows from this that one's conduct must correspond to the purpose for which one was created (*T. Naph.* 2.9), and that those who depart from God's law (as the Gentiles have) are forsaking "the Lord" (God) and disrupting the created order (*T. Naph.* 3.2–4).

In part, this is Paul's argument, too. Food and the stomach can only fulfill their respective roles when they do so in relation to one another. Similarly, the body is only itself when it acts in accord with its relationship to Christ, and Christ is Lord in so far as he is present as Lord for those who belong to him.[16] Yet for Paul, a person's relationship to Christ is inaugurated not at creation but at the new creation, with baptism; and in receiving the Spirit (v. 19; cf. 2.12) the believer "is involved with the Lord" and becomes "one spirit with him" (v. 17; cf. 12.12–13). Accordingly, the apostle's summons is not to obey the law, or even to "obey" the Lord, but to act in ways that are appropriate to the new reality of one's life in Christ.[17] This means that the Lord is "for" the body in a way that the body cannot be "for" the Lord, as a transforming and enlivening presence, a gift no less than a claim. The ultimate expression of this lordship is to come at "the end," when Christ will claim the resurrected body (v. 14), wholly and without reservation, for the reign of God (15.24–28).[18]

One also needs to consider how Paul moves from his premise about the body's belonging to the Lord (6.13b) to his appeal, "Distance yourselves from sexual immorality" (v. 18a), and why he distinguishes *porneia* as an offense that is committed "against one's

---

[14] E.g., C. K. Barrett, *The First Epistle to the Corinthians*, BNTC (London, 1968), 146–47; Fee, *First Epistle*, 253–55; Schrage, *Der erste Brief*, II.10–11, 20.   [15] *Die Sünde*, 128–29.

[16] See Kirchhoff, *Die Sünde*, 124–25.

[17] Similarly, ibid., 125–30; Schrage, *Der erste Brief*, II.23–24.

[18] Cf. Käsemann, "Anthropology," 21–22.

own body" (v. 19). His move from premise to appeal is most visible in verses 15–17, where he illustrates the problem with *porneia* by referring to a man – he means any man – who takes up with a prostitute. Now describing the "bodies" of believers as "members of Christ," he rules out as unthinkable making these also "members of a prostitute" (v. 15). It is not the sexual relationship as such that is the problem, or Paul could not approve of sexual union within a marriage, as he does in chapter 7 (e.g., vv. 2–4, 5, 9, 28, 36). The problem is that having sex with a prostitute manifests an orientation toward sexual immorality in general, which the apostle repeatedly associates with idolatry (5.10, 11; 6.9, 10; 10.7–8). Therefore, anyone who goes to a prostitute has deserted the realm where Christ is Lord for the death-dealing chaos of a realm that is ruled by many "so-called" gods and lords (cf. 8.5). These two realms are also in view when he comments that "the man who is involved with a prostitute is one body with her" (v. 16, citing Gen. 2.24 about being "one flesh" with a woman), and that "the person who is involved with the Lord is one spirit with him" (v. 17). In each case he is referring to a relationship that stamps one's life as a whole, gives it a particular direction, and therefore claims it exclusively.[19]

The Lord's claim is established at baptism when the believer becomes "one spirit with him" (v. 17). Baptism is also the occasion for God's giving of the Holy Spirit, through whose working the believer's body becomes a "temple" in which the Spirit dwells (v. 19a; cf. 12.12–13; 2.12). Because in this way God's temple is erected in the profane world, for those who belong to the Lord there are no longer any special sacred places.[20] Believers have been "sanctified [and] called" (1.2) to serve God in the places they already inhabit (cf. 7.17–24). Their bodies, now enlivened by the Spirit, ruled by the Lord, and no longer their "own" (v. 19b), are the agents for this service. Therefore, when Paul identifies *porneia* as an offense that is "against one's own body" (v. 18c) he is referring to the "body" which, since baptism, belongs to the Lord, has been consecrated for the service of God, and is destined for resurrection. His remark that

---

[19] For discussions of the verb *kollasthai*, which I have translated as "involved with," and of the expressions "one body," "one flesh," and "one spirit," see Kirchhoff, *Die Sünde*, 158–76, and Schrage, *Der erste Brief*, II.26–30.

[20] Käsemann, "1. Korinther 6,19–20," 278.

"every [other] offense a person commits is outside the body" (v. 18b) is best explained as hyperbole, reflecting a belief that *porneia* is an especially serious violation of one's humanity.[21] For Paul, sexual immorality represents a "deeding" of one's whole body to the rule of other lords, which is idolatry. It therefore desecrates God's temple, offends against God's Holy Spirit, and violates the life that God has given.[22]

The apostle summarizes his point in v. 20, where, typically, his imperative is founded on an indicative: "Because you were bought and paid for, therefore glorify God in your body." With the metaphor of purchase Paul is portraying believers as slaves who, since their baptism, have a new master. This extends the metaphor of ownership that is implied in the preceding remark, "you are not your own" (v. 19c). The unnamed purchaser is the Lord, in whom believers have their life and by whom their lives ("bodies") are claimed for the service of God. However, the apostle shows no interest in the "transaction" itself – for example, from whom believers have been purchased or for what price. In this context his single point is that the baptized now belong exclusively to the Lord. Even if he means that they belong to him as "freed persons" (*apeleutheroi*; see 7.22–23), the relationship nonetheless involves obligations as well as benefits, just as even an ex-slave in Paul's day continued in a client relationship either to a former master or to some other patron.[23]

A believer's obligations are summed up in the appeal to "glorify God in your body" (v. 20b). With this the temple metaphor is carried a step farther. Because the body is God's temple, whatever one does in the body should redound to God's glory. God is glorified as God is affirmed, not only in the prayers and praise of the church's worship, but also in the faithful service of God, both individual and corporate, that manifests itself in daily life. The appeal is therefore comprehensive, as in 10.31, and may be taken

---

[21] Brendan Byrne, "Sinning against One's Own Body: Paul's Understanding of the Sexual Relationship in 1 Corinthians 6:18," *CBQ* 45 (1983), 608–16; Schrage, *Der erste Brief*, II.31–33.

[22] Similarly, Kirchhoff, *Die Sünde*, 177–88; cf. Fee, *First Epistle*, 262–63; Schrage, *Der erste Brief*, II.31, 33–34.

[23] The social background of the metaphor is discussed by Dale B. Martin, *Slavery as Salvation: The Metaphor of Slavery in Pauline Christianity* (New Haven, CT, 1990), 63–68, esp.

as a positive form of the call to distance oneself from sexual immorality. Those who do not glorify God are forsaking God and falling into idolatry (thus Ps. 106.19–23; Jer. 2.11, echoed in Rom. 1.21–23), which is exactly what *porneia* represents.

Responding to God's call

The principal directive in 7.17–24 is that ordinarily believers should remain in the social settings and relationships within which they first heard and responded to the gospel (vv. 20, 24). With this Paul is both supporting and generalizing the counsels about marriage, singleness, and divorce which precede (vv. 1–16) and follow (vv. 25–40). His comments in these intervening verses are connected most directly with the preceding advice that a believer who has an unbelieving spouse should nonetheless remain in that marriage (vv. 12–16).[24] Paul allows for exceptions, however, recognizing that sometimes a divorce will be sought by the unbelieving spouse. In such a case the believer should consent, because "it is to peace that God has called you" (v. 15, NRSV). Following on from this mention of God's call, the apostle proceeds with the general instruction that, whatever the specifics of their individual situations, believers are always to live "as the Lord has apportioned to each one, and as God has called each one" (v. 17a).

This directive and the ones it introduces presuppose what Paul has been affirming since the opening lines of the letter: believers have been called of God to belong to Christ (e.g., 1.2, 9, 24, 26, 30; 3.23; 6.12–20). This is now expressed in the statement that any slave "who was called in the Lord" has become "a freed person of the Lord" (v. 22a), and that any free person who was called has become "a slave of Christ" (v. 22b). To underscore this bond between believers and the Lord Paul refers metaphorically (as in 6.20a) to a purchase price: believers belong to the Lord just as surely and fully as slaves belong to the masters by whom they have been "bought and paid for" (v. 23a).

The apostle takes specific account of the fact that God's call to belong to Christ is necessarily received within the concrete realities

---

[24] Fee, *First Epistle*, 307; Schrage, *Der erste Brief*, II.129.

of particular social situations (cf. 1.26–29), and that one person's circumstances are never exactly the same as another's. His own counsels here in chapter 7 afford glimpses of the diverse domestic situations of those in Corinth who have accepted the gospel: some were married, some had never been married; some were betrothed, others widowed, others divorced; in some cases the spouse or betrothed has also accepted the gospel, in other cases one of the two remains an unbeliever. Now, generalizing from his counsels about these situations, he offers two more examples: God has called both circumcised and uncircumcised (vv. 18–19), and both slaves and free (vv. 21–23).[25] These are the types of specific social situations that Paul has in view when he directs the Corinthians to "remain in the calling in which you were called" (v. 20).[26] Repeating this a few lines later he expresses himself more exactly: they are to "remain there with God" (v. 24). Just as the believer's own place is always the very first place where God is known, so it is always the very first place where God is to be served.

In this counsel to serve in the place where God's call has been received, living in accordance with that call and "as the Lord has apportioned," there is no thought of either capitulation or resignation to the status quo. Believers are conditioned but not claimed by their particular circumstances. They gain their identity not from who or where they happen to be within society but from who they are in their belonging to Christ (vv. 18–19a, 21a, 22–23). Those who are claimed by the Lord are in principle free from the claims of the world ("don't become slaves of any human beings," v. 23b; cf. 3.21–23) and free for "keeping God's commandments" (v. 19b). In this context, "keeping God's commandments" means leading one's life in accordance with God's call (v. 17a), as one who belongs to Christ (v. 22) – just as later on in the

---

[25] These further examples probably reflect Paul's acquaintance with the baptismal declaration that is present, perhaps close to its original form, in Gal. 3.28, and that also lies behind 1 Cor. 12.13. However, the reference to male and female that stands in Galatians does not appear in 1 Corinthians, conceivably because it was being misinterpreted by some people in the Corinthian church (see the commentaries).

[26] In v. 20 the noun "calling" (*klēsis*) does not refer to God's act of calling, but to the setting in which God's call was received (Barrett, *First Epistle*, 169–70; Schrage, *Der erste Brief*, II.137).

letter Paul will describe himself as being "in-lawed to Christ" (9.21).[27]

The apostle does not specify what "the Lord has apportioned to each one" (v. 17a). He probably does not mean, except perhaps secondarily, the believer's particular social circumstances at the time of his or her call,[28] because in this very passage he is emphasizing that it makes little difference what those circumstances were. More likely, he is thinking primarily of the particular and differing gifts with which believers are endowed for leading the life to which each has been called.[29] This interpretation accords better with his view of the relative insignificance of one's situation in the world. It is also in keeping with his remark earlier in this same context, that "each [believer] has a particular gift from God, one of one kind and another of a different kind" (v. 7b).[30] As a result, there is no uniform way for believers to lead their lives according to God's call. Because their gifts and their circumstances are different, so are their opportunities and responsibilities.

Finally, Paul is not saying that one is obliged *in principle* to remain in the situation where God's call has been received. This is evident from the wider context in chapter 7, where he allows for circumstances in which it might be advisable for a single or widowed believer to marry (vv. 9, 28, 36, 38, 39), a divorced believer to re-marry (v. 11), or a married believer to divorce (v. 15). It is also and more immediately evident in his counsel to slaves. If, in fact, they are able to gain their freedom, they should seize the opportunity (v. 21b).[31]

For Paul, the sum of the matter is this: although the concrete

---

[27] Note, as well, the parallels in Gal. 5.6 (where what matters most is "faith rendered active through love") and 6.15 (where what matters most is "a new creation"). On the expression, "in-lawed to Christ," see Furnish, "Belonging to Christ: A Paradigm for Ethics in First Corinthians," *Interp* 44 (1990), 155–56, and "Theology in 1 Corinthians," *Pauline Theology* II, 59–89, here: 85.   [28] Thus Fee, *First Epistle*, 310; cf. Barrett, *First Epistle*, 168.

[29] Friedrich Lang, *Die Briefe an die Korinther*, NTD 7 (Göttingen and Zürich, 1986), 96; Schrage, *Der erste Brief*, II.133; similarly, Hans Conzelmann, *1 Corinthians*, Hermeneia (Philadelphia, 1975), 125–26.

[30] Note, in addition, Paul's later reference to the Spirit's distribution of various gifts (12.11), and his statement in Rom. 12.3 about "the measure of faith" that God "has apportioned" to each (*emerisen*, as in 1 Cor. 7.17a).

[31] The arguments for this interpretation are compelling. See esp., J. Albert Harrill, *The Manumission of Slaves in Early Christianity*, HUT 32 (Tübingen, 1995), 68–128; also, e.g., Fee, *First Epistle*, 317–18; Schrage, *Der erste Brief*, II.139–40.

social realities of believers' lives may remain the same, in belonging to Christ their relationship to those realities is radically changed. Exactly *how* their new life in Christ will be reflected in their daily lives will vary, depending both on their individual circumstances and on the particular gifts that each has been granted. However, what is most fundamentally true about their call is true for all. They are no longer identified or claimed in any ultimate sense by their situation in the world, but now and decisively by their belonging to Christ.

Dealings with the world

In 7.29–35, following his comments about responding to God's call in the situation where it was received (vv. 17–24), the apostle resumes his counsels about the advisability of marriage by taking up the situation of those who have never been married (v. 25). Invoking the principle he has just articulated (vv. 20, 24), he says that "one does well to stay as one is" (v. 26a). Therefore, just as a man who is married should stay with his wife (v. 27a; cf. vv. 10–11), so an unmarried man should not go looking for one (v. 27b; cf. v. 8). Again, as in vv. 17–24, in the process of supporting his counsels the apostle generalizes them; and again, this sheds light on the theological standpoint from which he is writing. Specifically, we are able to catch a glimpse of the eschatological expectation that informs these counsels, and of how this expectation relates to his views about belonging to Christ.[32]

Certain of Paul's eschatological expectations have been evident since the beginning of this letter. He has already referred, in various contexts, to Christ's "revealing" at the last day (1.7–8) and to the coming judgment (3.13–15; 4.4–5; 5.5, 13), resurrection of the

---

[32] Representative studies of 7.29–35: Wolfgang Schrage, "Die Stellung zur Welt bei Paulus, Epiktet und in der Apokalyptik. Ein Beitrag zu 1Kor 7,29–31," *ZTK* 1 (1964), 125–54; Herbert Braun, "Die Indifferenz gegenüber der Welt bei Paulus und bei Epiktet," *Gesammelte Studien zum Neuen Testament und seiner Welt* (2nd edn.; Tübingen, 1967), 159–67; Darrell J. Doughty, "The Presence and Future of Salvation in Corinth," *ZNW* 66 (1975), 61–90; David L. Balch, "1 Cor 7:32–35 and Stoic Debates About Marriage, Anxiety, and Distraction," *JBL* 102 (1983), 429–39; Vincent L. Wimbush, *Paul, the Worldly Ascetic: Response to the World and Self-Understanding according to 1 Corinthians 7* (Macon, GA, 1987); Will Deming, *Paul on marriage and celibacy: The Hellenistic background of 1 Corinthians 7*, SNTSMS 83 (Cambridge, 1995), esp. 173–205.

dead (6.14), and reign of God (4.20; 6.9–10). When he now comments that "the time is compressed" (v. 29a) and that "this visible world is passing away" (v. 31b), he means that the end of this age is already being experienced (note 10.11). It is in this connection that Paul's reference to "the impending necessity" is to be understood (v. 26a). In accord with traditional apocalyptic expectations, he seems to be anticipating that there will be all kinds of cosmic havoc and social turmoil as the end draws ever nearer, and that this will create especially difficult circumstances for women and infants (see, e.g., Dan. 12.1; *1 Enoch* 99.5; 2 Esd. 4.51–5.13; 6.18–24; Rev. 7.14; Mark 13.17–19; Luke 23.27–29).[33] Thus one of his reasons for advising the unmarried to remain so, is to spare them the additional "distress in this life" (v. 28c, NRSV) that those who are married will experience in the last days.

Paul's statements about the compression of time and the passing away of this present age frame and support five particularly significant instructions (vv. 29b–31a): "Let those who have wives be as not having them, and those who sorrow as not sorrowing, and those who rejoice as not rejoicing, and those who buy as not owning, and those who are occupied with the world as not preoccupied with it." There are two premises that underlie and support these counsels, one of them eschatological and the other christological. The eschatological premise, which is made explicit in the framing statements, is that *"the time" has grown short and everything that constitutes this world is even now passing away.* The christological premise is implicit in the following verses, which show how concerned Paul is that believers be devoted to the Lord "without distractions" (vv. 32–35). In earlier chapters, and as recently as v. 22 in this one, it has been quite explicit: *believers have been claimed by the Lord, and in their belonging to him they have been granted a new identity and status.* These two premises are inseparably related. "The time" (*ho kairos*) to which Paul refers (v. 29a) is the interval between Christ's resurrection and his

---

[33] This is the view of most commentators (e.g., Conzelmann, *1 Corinthians*, 132; Barrett, *First Epistle*, 175; Lang, *Korinther*, 99; Schrage, *Der erste Brief*, II.156–57), although Fee (*First Epistle*, 329) argues for a more general meaning. Even if Paul's reference in v. 26 is to a *"present* necessity" (the translation, "impending," is disputed), an eschatological interpretation of the phrase is still the most plausible. It is supported both by the statement that "this visible world is [in the process of] passing away" (31b) and by a later remark that "the ends of the ages have come" (10.11, NRSV).

"revealing." What is fast approaching is therefore nothing else than the return of the Lord by whom believers have been claimed and graced with new life. At least in this context, Paul's eschatology is christologically focused.[34]

The "as not" statements which derive from these two premises are sometimes described as advising the Corinthians to remain "aloof" from their earthly circumstances, or at least to remain "indifferent" to them. Such words must be used carefully, however, because the apostle is certainly not counseling his hearers to withdraw from their responsibilities in society. In an earlier context he has dismissed this as a viable option (5.10), and in the present context he advises that, in general, those who belong to Christ ought to remain connected within the social situation where they received God's call (vv. 17–24, 26). Moreover, the "as not" instructions themselves presuppose both involvement in the world, even as it is passing away, and also the legitimacy of at least certain of the world's claims. Paul has already affirmed that a husband and wife are mutually obligated in the matter of sex (vv. 2–5). Now, even as he suggests that their many cares for one another will distract them from serving the Lord, it is evident that he regards this caring as both legitimate and proper to their marriage relationship (vv. 32–34).

It may be better to describe the "as not" statements as commending *detachment* from the world,[35] although certainly not in the form of an ascetic denying or demonizing of it. Indeed, the last and most general of these instructions suggests how all of them are to be understood: "those who are occupied with the world [should be] as not *pre*occupied with it" (v. 31a). In Paul's view, belonging to the Lord profoundly *changes* one's relationship to the world and to all of its social structures and institutions. Believers are no longer to regard the world as either the source of their life or the ground of their hope – hence, "no longer . . . as the sphere of human self assertion."[36] Their new relationship to the world is dialectical: even

[34] Cf. Wolfgang Schrage, *The Ethics of the New Testament* (Philadelphia, 1988), 182; *Der erste Brief*, II.167–68, 183.

[35] Archibald T. Robertson and Alfred Plummer, *A Critical and Exegetical Commentary on the First Epistle of St Paul to the Corinthians*, ICC (2d edn.; Edinburgh, 1914), 155.

[36] Doughty, "Presence and Future," 72.

as they continue to live and work in the very same places and positions as before their conversion, they are now there as people who have been given life in Christ and whose hope is in God.[37] This changed relationship to the world is more radical and of more consequence than any mere change of one's situation in the world could ever be. Since believers belong no longer to this age but to the Lord, the world's claims no longer exercise definitive control over their lives (3.21–23). But equally, because in their belonging to Christ they are already claimed for God's reign, even the present and transitory age has become for them "the sphere of Christian responsibility."[38]

Knowing as being known

Within the few lines that comprise 8.1–6 weighty assertions about knowledge and love are combined with the declaration that "for us" there is just "one God . . . and one Lord." From a rhetorical point of view these statements introduce Paul's response to one of the claims of religious privilege being made in his Corinthian congregation (8.7–11.1). In doing so, they not only lay the theological groundwork for that response but form the theological pivot on which the argument of this entire letter turns.

The particular issue calling for response is whether Christians are at liberty to eat meat that has come from pagan sacrificial rites. Customarily, meat left over from those rites was either served at a meal in the temple's dining room or else sold in a local market.[39] Like the matters Paul has addressed in chapters 5–7, this question reflects the difficulties faced by those who understand themselves as called to belong to Christ but who must still be very much

---

[37] Cf. Schrage, *Ethics*, 182, 202; *Der erste Brief*, II.173–74, 183.

[38] Doughty, "Presence and Future," 67.

[39] For details, including the pertinent archaeological evidence from Roman Corinth, see, e.g., Theissen, *Social Setting*, 121–43; Wendell Lee Willis, *Idol Meat in Corinth: The Pauline Argument in 1 Corinthians 8 and 10*, SBLDS 68 (Chico, CA, 1985), here: 7–64; Schrage, *Der erste Brief*, II.216–20; Richard E. Oster, "Use, Misuse and Neglect of Archaeological Evidence in Some Modern Works on 1Corinthians (1Cor 7,1–5; 8, 10; 11,2–16; 12,14–26," *ZNW* 83 (1992), 52–73, here: 64–66; Peter D. Gooch, *Dangerous Food: 1 Corinthians 8–10 in Its Context*, Studies in Christianity and Judaism, 5 (Waterloo, Ontario, 1993), here: 1–46; Justin J. Meggitt, "Meat Consumption and Social Conflict in Corinth," *JTS* 45 (1994), 137–41.

involved with an unbelieving society. Should believers avoid buying meat that has come from a pagan temple? Should they refuse to dine in temple restaurants? Should they decline invitations to eat in public establishments and the homes of non-Christian friends or family members where temple meat might be served? Paul's most direct responses to these questions are in 8.7–13 and 10.23–11.1, but what he says about his apostolic practice in chapter 9, and also his warnings concerning idolatry in 10.1–22, are by no means beside the point.[40]

Counsels and cautions

Paul agrees in principle with those Corinthian Christians who claim that their knowledge about God (8.1) affords them the *exousia* ("right," "liberty," "privilege," 8.9) to partake of meat from pagan sacrifices. In this connection he himself refers to a "freedom" (*eleutheria*) that is not to be given up (10.29b). How could this meat be morally or spiritually contaminated when the deities from whose temples it comes are "gods" in name only (8.4, 5)? Believers may therefore eat whatever is sold in the market or served to them by unbelievers without the worry of its perhaps carrying some religious contagion (10.25, 27).

For Paul, however, there is more to consider about exercising this particular right than the Corinthians who are urging it seem to realize. Specifically, they must consider the situation of those fellow believers who are still "weak" in conscience, and be willing out of concern for them to abstain from eating temple meat (e.g., 10.28–29a). The "weak" he has in view are those whose new knowledge of God has not yet re-formed their lives and sensitivities fully enough to deliver them without remainder from the pagan beliefs they have so long and so recently held (8.7). He therefore cautions the stronger believers: "See to it that this right of yours doesn't become a stumbling block to those who are weak. For if someone should see you who have knowledge dining in an idol's temple, will

---

[40] Representative discussions (in addition to those in n. 39): Richard A. Horsley, "Consciousness and Freedom among the Corinthians: 1 Corinthians 8–10," *CBQ* 40 (1978), 574–89; Jerome Murphy-O'Connor, "Freedom or the Ghetto (1 Cor., VIII, 1–13; X, 23–XI, 1)," *RB* 85 (1978), 543–74; Meeks, "Polyphonic Ethics"; Borgen, "'Yes,' 'No'"; Thomas Söding, *Das Liebesgebot bei Paulus: Die Mahnung zur Agape im rahmen der paulinischen Ethik*, NTAbh, n. F. 26 (Münster, 1995), 102–24.

not that person, when weak in conscience, be 'built up' to eat what has been sacrificed to an idol?" (8.9b–10)

As in Romans 14.23, Paul means that where the weak are thus encouraged to violate their conscience, their eating cannot be an expression of faith but only of idolatry, and therefore sin. For this reason, and in a statement that is more emphatic for being cast hyperbolically, he offers his own firm resolve as an example: "If food causes my brother or sister to fall, I will certainly not eat meat, for all of eternity, in order not to cause my brother or sister to fall" (8.13). His personal example is also the point of chapter 9. As an apostle he has a well-established right (*exousia*) to get his livelihood from the churches (vv. 1–14), but he has not exercised this right, even though it involves the necessary "eating and drinking" (v. 4) that sustains life, lest it hinder his preaching of the gospel (vv. 15–27). How much more ought one to be willing to refrain from partaking of meat from pagan temples, whenever eating it could cause harm to the conscience of a fellow believer!

Paul supplements these counsels with warnings about the grave dangers of idolatry itself (10.1–22). His warnings both presuppose and call attention to an important distinction. The meat that has been left over from pagan rites poses no threat in and of itself, so believers are free in principle to eat it as they may choose (v. 19). However, believers are absolutely forbidden ever to participate as worshipers in pagan rites, because that would mean abandoning God for the demons (vv. 20–21), and thereby crossing a boundary that must not be crossed.[41] To make this point the apostle invokes Israel's experience in the wilderness, holding it up as a sober lesson for the church in an unbelieving society. Contrary to what some Corinthians suppose, neither baptism nor participation in the Lord's supper offers immunity from the punishment that God is sure to visit upon idolaters (vv. 1–5, 14–22): "So let the one who presumes to be standing be careful not to fall" (v. 12). The formulation here echoes an earlier caution directed to whoever "presumes to know something," but who "doesn't yet know as one must know" (8.2). In both cases, as throughout 8.1–11.1, Paul is concerned that

---

[41] Cf. Schrage, *Der erste Brief*, II.382, 444–45. It is unclear why Paul is now referring to the "so-called gods" (8.5) as "demons," but there is little doubt that he has the same false deities in mind (see 10.14, 19, and Borgen, "'Yes,' 'No,'" 40, n. 18).

those who are complacent in their "knowledge" about God and
attentive mainly to their own rights are putting the whole congregation at risk, and most especially the fragile faith of those who are
"weak."

Knowledge and love

Paul introduces the question about meat from pagan temples with
two affirmations that are of critical theological importance, one
about knowing God (8.1–3) and another about belonging to one
God and one Lord (vv. 4–6). In addition to forming the basis of the
counsels in 8.7–11.1, these two affirmations draw together various
theological strands that are definitive of the letter's overall theological orientation.

On both points the apostle is in dialogue with those members of
his congregation who have no scruples about eating meat sacrificed
to idols. Their claim to "knowledge," which he cites in vv. 1a, 4,
establishes a specifically theological basis for their position: since
they know that "there is no God but one," they can be confident
that the meat sacrificed in pagan temples has no religious
significance or potency and may be eaten with impunity. Paul of
course agrees with their belief in just one God, which derives from
his own missionary preaching (12.2; 1 Thess. 1.9–10; Gal. 4.8–9),
although he also seems to allow for the existence of certain
demonic powers (v. 5; cf. 10.20–21). He does not agree, however,
that "all" in the congregation (v. 1a) are well established in their
knowledge that God is one; the "weak" are not (see 8.7), and that
is the reason for his present concern.

The rhetorical climax of this introduction comes in v. 6, where
the apostle is probably citing, and perhaps to some extent adapting, a two-part creedal formulation:

> Yet for us there is one God, the Father,
>   from whom all things exist, and we exist for him;
> and there is one Lord, Jesus Christ,
>   through whom all things exist, and we exist through him.

The introductory "for us" and the use of the first person plural at
the end of each part invest this statement with an existential character that distinguishes it from all merely theoretical assertions. It

is not speculative but confessional. It is not just a statement of the church's *knowledge about* the one God and one Lord, but voices its *acknowledgment of* the one God and one Lord.[42]

In the first part of this creed (v. 6a) God is acknowledged as the Creator of "all things," meaning not that he is just the artificer of creation from some kind of primal matter, but that he is the actual source "from whom" (*ex hou*) all things come, where before there was nothing (cf. Rom. 4.17).[43] It is primarily for this reason, because he is the acknowledged generator of all life, that God is described here as "the Father." To the extent that his relationship to Christ (his "Son," 1.9; 15.28) may also be in view, that remains distinctly secondary, not expressed in either part of the creed. What comes to the fore is the relationship of *believers* to God, in the confessional statement that "we exist for him" (*eis auton*). With this the faithful community affirms that God is its future, the eschatological goal of human existence, the consummation as well as the origin of all things. This understanding of God as the one to whom all things belong (cf. 3.23; 15.24–28) provides the theological basis for the view, which the apostle shares with the stronger members of his congregation, that nothing, not even meat from pagan sacrifices, is in itself unclean (10.25–27; cf. Rom. 14.14a).

The two expressions of monotheism that Paul cites, one from the stronger believers in Corinth (v. 4) and one from a creed (v. 6a), both echo the *Shema Yisrael* of Jewish tradition, "Hear, O Israel, the Lord our God is one Lord" (Deut. 6.4, NRSVmg.). It is therefore all the more striking when the second part of the creed affirms that there is *also* "one Lord, Jesus Christ" (v. 6b). Here the title *kyrios*, which in the Greek version of Deuteronomy 6.4 belongs to the one and only God (*theos*), is used to affirm that Christ is the Lord. The result has been described as "a sort of

---

[42] Representative studies focused especially on the theological issues (see also n. 40): Jerome Murphy-O'Connor, "1 Cor. VIII, 6: Cosmology or Soteriology?" *RB* 85 (1978), 253–67; James D. G. Dunn, *Christology in the Making: A New Testament Inquiry into the Origins of the Doctrine of the Incarnation* (2nd edn.; Grand Rapids, 1996), 179–83; Traugott Holtz, "Theologie und Christologie bei Paulus," *Glaube und Eschatologie. Festschrift für Werner Georg Kümmel zum 80. Geburtstag* (ed. by E. Gräßer and O. Merk; Tübingen, 1985), 105–21; Wilhelm Thüsing, *Gott und Christus in der paulinischen Soteriologie. Vol.I: Per Christum in Deum. Das Verhältnis der Christozentrik zur Theozentrik*, NTAbh, n. F. 1/I (3rd edn.; Münster, 1986), 225–37, 280–90; Richardson, *Paul's Language about God*, 296–304.

[43] Schrage, *Der erste Brief*, II.242.

christological monotheism,"[44] yet the creed itself shows no concern for monotheism as a theory, and therefore simply allows the two statements to stand side by side. In acknowledging Christ as the one "through whom [*di' hou*] all things exist" and confessing that "we exist through him [*di' autou*]," the faithful community is affirming him as God's agent both in creation and in the new creation (salvation). God remains the source and the destiny of all existence (*ex hou . . . eis auton*), the one to whom all things belong. But just as surely, it is through Christ that believers have come to know God as the one who has called all things into existence, and who has called them into new life (cf. 1.30: "And from [God] you are in Christ Jesus" [*ex autou de hymeis este en Christō Iēsou*]).

By juxtaposing this two-part affirmation with his quotations of Corinthian claims to know about the one God, Paul is effectively subordinating a doctrinal truth, "monotheism," to the existential reality that "for us" knowing God involves *belonging* to the one God, wherein one is delivered from the reign of the so-called gods which has come to an end.[45] The reality is that one now belongs to the domain where Christ is Lord, to God's new creation which has been established through the cross – "through the foolishness of the kerygma" (1.21). Paul invokes this kerygma as he proceeds with his appeals on behalf of the weak. Because Christ died for them just as he did for the whole of humankind, they are not to be dismissed as "the weak" but affirmed and supported as "the brothers and sisters" (literally, "the brother," 8.11; and for emphasis, three more times in vv. 12, 13). What is decisive is not their uncertainty about God and the "gods," but the certainty that they are beneficiaries of God's saving power. Therefore, to sin against these brothers and sisters by destroying their faith is to sin against Christ himself (v. 12), because one is thereby violating God's new creation of which Christ is the agent.

This new creation is constituted by the saving power of God's *agapē* (love) that is disclosed and bestowed through Christ's death. This is the point of the stark contrast that Paul introduces in the

---

[44] N. Thomas Wright, *The Climax of the Covenant: Christ and the Law in Pauline Theology* (Minneapolis, 1992), 129.   [45] Cf. Schrage, *Der erste Brief*, II.241.

opening lines of his discussion: "Knowledge inflates, but love builds up. Whoever presumes to know something doesn't yet know as one must know; but whoever loves God has been known by him" (8.1b–3). The knowledge that "inflates" is the knowledge about God that some Corinthians claim to possess as a special gift (e.g., 1.5; 12.8), and then flaunt in the congregation as a sign of their religious privilege and superior status. But the knowledge that matters is the existential reality of *being known* by God. According to the scriptural tradition in which Paul is steeped, to be "known" by God means to be acknowledged and affirmed as God's own, embraced within a community that lives from God's grace and faithfulness, and called and claimed for the service of God.[46] How one "must know" God is by acknowledging the electing grace of God's prior "knowing," and allowing it to inhabit and shape one's life; in a word, by *loving* God.

The expression, "to love God," which Paul uses elsewhere only in 2.9 (a citation) and Romans 8.28, appears to have been a traditional Jewish theological formulation.[47] His use of it here is doubly appropriate. First, it helps to make the point that knowing God involves an existential relationship, not just acceptance of the proposition that "God is one." This, too, accords with the apostle's Jewish heritage, where knowing God is associated with such expressions as "fearing" (Prov. 1.7; 2.5; 1 Kgs. 8.43/2 Chr. 6.33; Isa. 11.2) and "serving" (1 Chr. 28.9; cf. Wis. 2.13) God, "trusting" in him (Ps. 9.10 [Hebrew v. 11]; Prov. 3.5–7; Isa. 43.10), and "cleaving" to him (Ps. 91.14).[48] Second, this formulation helps to emphasize the critical importance of love by identifying it with what is both given and required in being known by God. Those of stronger faith

---

[46] See Gen. 18.19; Exod. 33.12, 17; Num. 16.5; 2 Sam. 7.20/1 Chr. 17.18; Pss. 37.18; 139.1–6, 23–24; 144.3; Jer. 1.5; Hos. 13.5; Amos 3.2; in other Pauline letters, Rom. 8.28; 11.2; Gal. 4.9. Discussions by G. Johannes Botterweck, "יָדַע," *TDOT* 5, 449–81, here: 468–69; Rudolf Bultmann, "γινώσκω," *TDNT* I.689–719, here: 709–10; also Jacques Dupont, *Gnosis. La connaissance religieuse dans les épîtres des S. Paul* (2nd edn.; Louvain and Paris, 1960), 51–104; Ernst Baasland, "Cognitio Dei im Römerbrief," *SNTU*, 14 (1989), 185–218, here: 190–93.

[47] E.g., Sir. 1.10; 2.15, 16; 31.19; 47.22; *Pss. Sol.* 4.25; 6.6; 14.1; *1 Enoch* 108.8 (and also the Greek version of Judg. 5.31). See esp., Oda Wischmeyer, "ΘΕΟΝ ΑΓΑΠΑΝ bei Paulus. Eine traditionsgeschichtliche Miszelle," *ZNW* 78 (1987), 141–44.

[48] Botterweck, "יָדַע," 469–70; cf. James M. Ward, "The Servant's Knowledge in Isaiah 40–55," *Israelite Wisdom. Theological and Literary Essays in Honor of Samuel Terrien* (ed. by J. Gammie *et al.*; Missoula, MT, 1978), 121–36.

are to understand that the liberty they claim is only fulfilled when it is exercised in the love that inheres in God's call to belong to Christ. In 1.18–2.16 Paul emphasized that this call comes through the "foolish" wisdom of the cross. The contrast that he drew there between the world's wisdom and God's is now present again as he contrasts *having* knowledge that only inflates with *being* known by the upbuilding love of God.[49] With this it becomes clear that for Paul the saving power of God revealed in the cross is the power of God's self-giving love (cf. 2 Cor. 5.14; Rom. 5.8). This is the grace of which Christ is the agent (1.2, 3; cf. 8.6) and of which his cross is the sign (8.11).

Because God's self-giving, upbuilding love is constitutive of the new creation mediated through the cross, it is also the norm for life within this new creation. To "have the mind of Christ" (2.16) therefore means to be continually formed and informed by the *agapē* of which Christ's death is definitive. This is also the point of the quite general appeal with which Paul concludes his counsels in this part of the letter, "Be imitators of me, just as I am of Christ" (11.1). Earlier he had described his apostolic labors and hardships as, in effect, bearing the cruciform imprint of God's *agapē* (4.9–13, cf. v. 21). His comments in the present context about declining material support (9.15–18) and adapting his ministry to take account of the situations of those he would save (9.19–23) point to examples of this. Another example is his resolve not to eat meat from a pagan temple if doing so might injure the conscience of a brother or sister (8.13). He does not suggest in any of these cases that love has rescinded or even restricted one's freedom. Rather, he regards the freedom that comes with belonging to Christ as *fulfilled* in love. As an apostle "in-lawed to Christ" (*ennomos Christou*, 9.21) he can write, "*Being* free in every way, I have enslaved myself to everyone that I might win over the many" (9.19).[50] He views this putting aside of one's own interests for the sake of others (10.24, 33) as a working

---

[49] Similarly, Troels Engberg-Pedersen, "The Gospel and Social Practice according to I Corinthians," *NTS* 33 (1987), 557–84, here: 567.

[50] This causal interpretation of the participial clause, *eleutheros ōn*, accords better with Paul's overall thought about the freedom that inheres in belonging to Christ (e.g., Gal. 5.13–14) than the usual interpretation of it as concessive (e.g., NRSV: "For though I am free . . ."). Thus Schrage, *Der erste Brief*, II.338; also James Moffatt, *The First Epistle of Paul to the Corinthians*, MNTC (New York and London, 1938), 122.

out of the love revealed in the cross. This is a love that liberates from the bondage to oneself that would otherwise relentlessly diminish life by turning it away from its Creator and alienating it from the rest of God's creation.[51]

Although Paul does not specifically mention *agapē* again until chapter 13, its critical importance as the content of the saving power of God and therefore of the new creation is presupposed in the rest of the letter. This is clear from the specially formulated appeal to do everything in love, which seems intended as a summary of all the letter's counsels (16.14), from the apostle's ben-edictory conveyance of his *agapē* in the letter's subscript (16.24, unique to 1 Corinthians), and not least from his repeated calls for the congregation to apply itself to the "upbuilding" (*oikodomein, hē oikodomē*, 10.23; 14.3–5, 12, 17, 26) which love effects (8.1b). Knowledge, too, continues to be a theme, both the knowledge that the Spirit bestows on some believers in this age (12.8; 13.2, 8, 9; 14.6) and the profounder knowing that inheres in being known by God, but will be fulfilled only in the age to come (13.12).

---

[51] In Gal. 5.13–14 Paul writes of the love that actualizes freedom as also fulfilling the law, and then describes this *agapē* as "the law of Christ" (6.2; cf. 1 Cor. 9.21, "in-lawed to Christ").

CHAPTER 4

Belonging to Christ in a believing community

As we have seen, all of the issues Paul takes up in 1 Corinthians
5.1–11.1 arise from the fact that those who belong to Christ necessarily continue to be involved in various ways with an unbelieving
society. Although the difficulties and responsibilities of being an
end-time community with present-time involvements are still in
view in 11.2–14.40, the focus in this part of the letter is more on life
within the believing community itself. Here the apostle addresses
three matters that concern him about the congregation's conduct
when all of its members, each of whom would have been associated with some particular household conventicle, "assemble as a
church" (11.18) at one place (cf. 11.20; 14.23): the hair of women
who pray or prophesy should be properly arranged (11.3–16), the
"Lord's supper" should be observed in a manner that is appropriate to its significance (11.17–34), and spiritual gifts should be exercised in ways that benefit others (14.1–40).[1]

As in the preceding sections of the letter, the apostle supports his
directives primarily by emphasizing that, in their belonging to
Christ and to God, believers participate in a new order of existence
which both graces and claims their lives even while the present age
continues. This is most evident in 12.12–13.13, the letter's second
sustained section of theological exposition (cf. 1.18–2.16). Here

---

[1] With most interpreters, I remain unconvinced by arguments that 11.2–16 is a later, non-
Pauline interpolation. For arguments favoring the hypothesis, see, e.g., William O.
Walker, Jr., "1 Corinthians 11:2–16 and Paul's Views Regarding Women," *JBL* 94 (1975),
94–110; idem, "The Vocabulary of 1 Corinthians 11.3–16: Pauline or Non-Pauline?"
JSNT 35 (1989), 75–88; and O. Lamar Cope, "1 Cor 11:2–16: One Step Further," *JBL* 97
(1978), 435–36. For arguments against it, see, e.g., Jerome Murphy-O'Connor, "The Non-
Pauline Character of 1 Corinthians 11:2–16?" *JBL* 95 (1976), 615–21; idem, "1
Corinthians 11:2–16 Once Again," *CBQ* 50 (1988), 265–74.

Paul lays the theological groundwork for his instructions about spiritual gifts by portraying life in Christ as membership in "one body," and by stressing the critical importance of *agapē*. Similarly, in 11.23–26 he supports his directives about conduct at the Lord's supper by citing the traditional words of eucharistic institution, and then offers a comment that calls attention to what the community should be doing as it gathers at "the Lord's table" (10.21). We must examine each of these passages in turn and in context.

There is no doubt that Paul also means to provide a theological basis for his instructions about the hairstyle of women who pray or prophesy (see, esp., 11.3, 7–12), but in this case his argument is obscure, at least to modern interpreters, and it may well have seemed unsatisfactory even to the apostle himself. At any rate, in the end he abandons argument altogether by suggesting that if his directives are not followed the Corinthians will be departing from the convention that obtains in other congregations (v. 16). Nonetheless, two clarion notes sounded earlier in the letter are echoed even in these verses, and distinctly enough to show that he is still holding to the center of his gospel.

First, Paul's comments are predicated on belief in the sovereignty of God, the one from whom all things come (v. 12b, "all things are from God"; cf. 8.6) and to whom, through Christ, all things belong (v. 3, God is the "head" even of Christ; cf. 3.23). In what respect exactly he regards the man to be "head" of a woman is left unclear, in part because his subject is not woman's subordination (or man's authority) but the need for women who pray or prophesy to be appropriately coifed, perhaps as a sign of their authority (*exousia*).[2] Indeed, Paul runs the risk of sabotaging his own argument when he attests that their common dependence on God puts man and woman on an equal footing (vv. 11–12).[3] From his standpoint, all social arrangements (including hierarchies),

---

[2] In addition to discussions in the commentaries, see, e.g., Morna D. Hooker, "Authority on her Head: An Examination of I Cor. xi.10," *NTS* 10 (1964), 410–16, repr. in *From Adam to Christ. Essays on Paul* (Cambridge, 1990), 113–20; Elisabeth Schüssler Fiorenza, *In Memory of Her. A Feminist Theological Reconstruction of Christian Origins* (New York, 1984), 227–30; L. Ann Jervis, "'But I Want You to Know . . .': Paul's Midrashic Intertextual Response to the Corinthian Worshipers (1 Cor 11:2–16)," *JBL* 112 (1993), 231–46.

[3] For a similar view of both the complexity and the fragility of Paul's argument, see Schrage, *Ethics*, 224–25, and *Der erste Brief*, II.496, 519–20, 525.

whether they exist by design or default, are substantially relativized by reason of all things belonging finally to Christ and to God.

Second, when the apostle specifies that men and women have equal standing "in the Lord" (v. 11), one hears the echo of another note that has been sounded repeatedly throughout earlier chapters. Believers participate in the new reality of a domain where Christ alone is Lord (8.6; cf. 4.17; 7.39; 9.1, 2; 10.21), and where they have been bound over to his service (cf. 6.12–20; 7.22–23). However, this point, like the first, is more specifically and clearly present in the second part of chapter 11 and in chapters 12–14.

THE LORD'S TABLE

Paul's discussion of the Lord's supper (11.17–34) does not proceed as a theological exposition of the meaning of the event, but takes the form of counsels about how the church in Corinth should be observing it. He does not mince words in registering objections to what was reportedly going on there (vv. 17–22), and he ends up giving a direction that is no less specific than the one about women who pray or prophesy (vv. 33–34a). But in the process, both to justify his taking up the subject and to warrant his directive, he calls attention to the significance of the rite as he understands it (vv. 23–32).[4]

Working from the apostle's comments in vv. 17–22, it is possible to reconstruct in a general way what typically happened – at least,

---

[4] Important, representative studies of the passage: Günther Bornkamm, "Lord's Supper and Church in Paul," *Early Christian Experience* (New York and Evanston, 1969), 123–60; Troels Engberg-Pedersen, "Proclaiming the Lord's Death: 1 Corinthians 11:17–34 and the Forms of Paul's Theological Argument," *Pauline Theology* II, 103–32; Otfried Hofius, "The Lord's Supper and the Lord's Supper Tradition: Reflections on 1 Corinthians 11:23b–25," *One Loaf, One Cup: Ecumenical Studies of 1 Cor 11 and Other Eucharistic Texts*, New Gospel Studies, 6 (ed. by Ben F. Meyer; Macon, GA, 1993), 75–115; Käsemann, "Lord's Supper"; Hans-Josef Klauck, "Presence in the Lord's Supper: 1 Corinthians 11:23–26 in the Context of Hellenistic Religious History," *One Loaf, One Cup: Ecumenical Studies of 1 Cor 11 and Other Eucharistic Texts*, New Gospel Studies, 6 (ed. by Ben F. Meyer; Macon, GA, 1993), 57–74; Peter Lampe, "Das korinthische Herrenmahl im Schnittpunkt hellenistisch-römischer Mahlpraxis und paulinischer Theologia Crucis (1Kor 11,17–34)," *ZNW* 82 (1991), 183–213; idem, "The Eucharist: Identifying with Christ on the Cross," *Interp* 48 (1994), 36–49; Theissen, *Social Setting*, 145–74. See also: Stephen C. Barton, "Paul's Sense of Place: An Anthropological Approach to Community Formation in Corinth," *NTS* 32 (1986), 225–46; Murphy-O'Connor, *St. Paul's Corinth*, 161–69.

according to reports reaching Paul (v. 18) – when the various house-churches of Corinth assembled as one to observe the Lord's supper. First, their ritual sharing of bread and cup took place in connection with an ordinary meal consisting of food brought along by the participants themselves. It appears that there were two separate ritual actions, the sharing of a common loaf likely occurring before the meal, and the sharing of a common cup at its conclusion.[5] Second, on these occasions certain "splits" (*schismata*, v. 18) and "distinctions" (*haireseis*, v. 19) were showing up among the church's members. Third, this cliquish behavior perhaps reflected significant differences of social and economic status; thus members who brought nothing with them for the meal (presumably the poorer) were being humiliated and going hungry, while those who could bring plenty to eat and drink (presumably the better off) enjoyed their own food, apparently without sharing it (vv. 21–22). What should have been an inclusive community meal had become an occasion for simultaneous private meals.[6] It is possible that these were taking place even before the poorer members were able to arrive, and thus before the ritual sharing of bread, although the evidence for this is not as secure as some interpreters suggest.[7]

Whether one translates Paul's directive in v. 33 as "wait for one another" (NRSV) or "care for one another,"[8] the basic point is the same: the congregation is not really participating in *the Lord's* supper as long as those who have more than enough to eat and drink disregard and thereby demean those who have little or nothing. Here the principle that Paul had applied to the case of "the weak" (8.1–11.1) is still operative: "You shouldn't each be looking out for yourself, but for the other person" (10.24); and also his comprehensive appeal, "Whether you eat, whether you drink, whatever you do,

---

[5] The evidence and arguments for this sequence are presented by Hofius, "The Lord's Supper," 80–88.

[6] Cf. Theissen, *Social Setting*, 147–63 – where, however, the social situation is spelled out in more detail than the evidence warrants.

[7] A decision in this matter depends mainly on the translation of the verb *prolambanei* in v. 21. Is this an instance where the word retains its temporal force (thus NRSV: "each of you *goes ahead* with your own supper"), or where that force has receded (thus REB, "each of you *takes* his own supper")? If Paul's instruction in v. 33 is best translated as "*wait [ekde-chesthe]* for one another" (both NRSV and REB), that could argue for the former, but Hofius ("The Lord's Supper," 93–95) has made a plausible case for translating it, instead, as "*care* for one another."   [8] See preceding note.

do everything to the glory of God" (10.31). In the present instance, however, there is something else to notice. The rather general instruction to be attentive to one another is followed by the proviso, "If someone is hungry, let that person eat at home . . ." (v. 34a). This is more specific than the rule to which it is attached, and it also corresponds to an earlier rhetorical question, "Don't you have homes for eating and drinking?" (v. 22a). Clearly, then, for Paul it is not the ordinary meal that defines the occasion but the two sacred actions of sharing the bread and sharing the cup. This is also evident from vv. 23–32, where he provides theological warrants both for the directive that will follow and for his complaint that the Corinthians are not in fact partaking of a *kyriakon deipnon* – that is, a supper that really does belong to the Lord (v. 20).

In order to show what distinguishes this supper of the Lord from an ordinary meal, the apostle cites a church tradition about its founding (vv. 23–25), adding an explanatory comment of his own (v. 26). How the version of the tradition he cites is related historically to those in the Synoptic Gospels, and whether he himself may have altered it for the present context, are complex questions which admit of no certain answers. In any event, for our purposes the more important question is how Paul understands this tradition and wants his congregation to understand it.

The tradition conveys both *actions* and *sayings* of "the Lord Jesus," and because these are introduced as dating from "the night he was betrayed" (v. 23b), one knows from the outset that they concern his death. At the same time, however, they are presented as the actions and sayings of "*the Lord* Jesus," the risen and exalted one. It is the "Lord's supper" about which Paul is writing (v. 20); he identifies the tradition as "from the Lord" (v. 23a); subsequently, he refers to "the death of the Lord" (v. 26), "the cup of the Lord" (v. 27), "the body and blood of the Lord" (v. 27), and being judged "by the Lord" (v. 32). The tradition does not invite the community simply to remember a figure from its past, but to celebrate the presence of its risen Lord.

Accordingly, although the opening words suggest that Jesus' actions are about to be described in some detail – he "took bread, and after he had given thanks he broke it" (vv. 23b–24a) – this turns out not to be the case. Subsequently, there is only an allusion to his actions with the cup ("Likewise [*hōsautōs*] also the cup . . .," v. 25a). Moreover and more importantly, the central and decisive action, which is Jesus' *giving* of the bread and the cup to the believing community, is not described at all but must be inferred from the accompanying sayings. Precisely by not describing this, the tradition both sets it apart from the preliminary actions and avoids confining it to the category of an event that lies only in the past.

The sayings that accompany the giving of the bread and the cup are of two kinds. In each instance a statement (indicative) is followed by an instruction (imperative).

The *statements* present the bread as the Lord's "body" and the cup/wine as "the new covenant" in his blood (vv. 24, 25), thereby identifying these everyday comestibles with the crucified one himself. In the first case, the bread is presented as the Lord's body "for you" (v. 24), meaning for the community as a whole (plural, *hymōn*). Here the assembled company is graced with both the presence of the Lord and the saving power of his death. However, neither the tradition itself nor Paul in citing it indicates how the phrase "for you" is to be interpreted. Is it to be understood in its most general sense, as "for your sake"? Or more particularly, as "for your sins" (see 15.3)? Or even quite specifically, as "in your place"? The open-ended statement allows for any of these meanings, or for all of them at once. In the second case, the Lord presents the cup as "the new covenant" established through his blood. The reference to blood is simultaneously a reference to life (thus Gen. 9.4; Lev. 17.11, 14; Deut. 12.23, etc.; cf. John 6.53, 54), and in this context summons the idea of a life that is given for others. But again, this is not spelled out, and nothing is said about the content of the new covenant that has been established through this gift of life (an allusion to Jer. 31.31–34 is by no means certain[9]). These formulas are focused on just one point. Nothing is allowed to draw attention away from the saving event itself, which is the death and continuing presence of "the Lord Jesus."

It is in keeping with this that the Lord's words are not explanatory statements but words of *bestowal*. They do not simply offer

---

[9] See, e.g., Christian Wolff, *Jeremia im Frühjudentum und Urchristentum*, TU 118 (Berlin, 1976), 116–47, and *Der erste Brief des Paulus an die Korinther*, THKNT 7 (Berlin, 1996), 268.

comments about the actions they accompany but are fully integral
to them. *In* those actions the Lord who speaks is giving *himself* ("*my*
body . . . for you," "the new covenant in *my* blood"). This absolute
bonding of action and word reflects the bonding of the gift to the
Giver. There is some reason to think that not all the members of
the Corinthian church appreciated this. Considering what Paul
says about the Israelites' experience in the wilderness when he
warns his congregation not to follow *their* example (10.1–5), the prevailing view in Corinth may have been that both baptism and the
bread and wine of the Lord's supper transmit a spiritual potency
that somehow guarantees divine favor. But in the tradition as Paul
conveys it here, the bread and the cup represent the Lord's giving
of *himself*, and thereby affirm his own saving presence.

For this reason, too, the *instructions* that accompany the actions
are not of the kind found, for example, in Matthew, which direct
the assembled company to "take" and "eat" the bread and to
"drink from [the cup]" (26.26, 27). Rather, in Paul's version of the
tradition, where in each case the instruction is the same, attention
is directed beyond the particulars of bread and cup to the
significance of the event as a whole: "Do this in remembrance of
me" (vv. 24, 25). The imperative to "do this" (*touto poieite*) pertains
to an *enactment* that transcends the ritual eating and drinking, and
the call to do this "in remembrance" of the Lord (*eis tēn emēn
anamnēsin*) summons the participants to receive the life that is given
through the Lord's saving death. Here, as in ancient Israel and formative Judaism, the community's remembering allows the past to
be powerfully and effectively *present*, defining, forming, and nour-
ishing its life.[10]

This call to remembrance does not appear at all in the Markan
or Matthean versions of the eucharistic tradition, and in Luke it
appears only in connection with the saying about the bread (22.19).
It may be that Paul himself has added this instruction to the cup-
saying (1 Cor. 11.25), just as he has probably added the stipulation
that the remembering should be "as often as" (*hosakis*) the community drinks of the ritual cup. Indeed, immediately following this

---

[10] See, e.g., Nils A. Dahl, "Anamnesis: Memory and Commemoration in Early
Christianity," *Jesus in the Memory of the Early Church* (Minneapolis, 1976), 11–29; Hermann
Patsch, "ἀνάμνησις," *EDNT* I.85–86.

expanded instruction he uses the same adverbial expression to introduce his own interpretive comment on the tradition: "For as often as [*hosakis*] you eat this bread and drink the cup it is the death of the Lord you are proclaiming, until he comes" (v. 26). Two matters deserve particular attention: the apostle's association of the church's eucharistic "remembrance" with its proclaiming of the Lord's death, and his reference to the Lord's expected return.

The main point of Paul's statement is that the community's remembering, as it gathers at the Lord's table, constitutes more than a renewal of its own sense of the Lord's continuing, saving presence. In being repeatedly reconstituted as a community that lives from his cross and manifests its meaning, those who share in the ritual bread and cup are simultaneously *proclaiming* the Lord's death. It is unlikely that the apostle associates this proclamation only with the words that are spoken in the eucharistic prayers or formulas.[11] More likely, his statement is about the entire occasion. Just as the community's remembering is identified with the celebration as a whole (the *doing* as well as the *saying*), so the celebration as a whole ("as often as you eat this bread and drink the cup") proclaims the Lord's death.[12] Paul ordinarily uses the verb "proclaim" (*katangellein*), as he has earlier in this letter (2.1; 9.14), with reference to preaching the gospel to non-believers, who would probably not have been present for the community's eucharistic celebration. When, despite this, he describes the sacramental act as "proclaiming" the death of the Lord – which is to say, his life-giving death *for others* – it is clear why he believes that the Corinthian church is not really observing the *Lord's* supper (11.20). Instead of demonstrating the new life that is established in the gift and claim of the cross, its celebrations demonstrate, rather, that considerations of social status continue to prevail even among those who profess to belong to the company of Christ.

The apostle's emphatic identification of the celebration as proclaiming the Lord's *death* may well have seemed strange, if not

---

[11] Thus Hofius, "The Lord's Supper," 108 (the eucharistic prayers); Fee, *First Epistle*, 557 (the bread and cup sayings); Lang, *Korinther*, 154 (either the bread and cup sayings or a eucharistic prayer).

[12] See, esp., Beverly Roberts Gaventa, "'You Proclaim the Lord's Death': 1 Corinthians 11:26 and Paul's Understanding of Worship," *RevExp* 80 (1983), 377–87; also, Bornkamm, "Lord's Supper," 141; Lampe, "Das korinthische Herrenmahl," 208–209; Engberg-Pedersen, "Proclaiming the Lord's Death," 115.

perverse, to any in Corinth who supposed they were somehow reigning already with "the Lord of glory" (4.8; 2.8). Thus the Corinthian point of view would also have been challenged by the apostle's remark that the community was to continue its eucharistic remembrance, and therefore its proclamation of the Lord's death, "until he comes." Paradoxically, for Paul the Lord who is *present* and known as the host of the table is also known as the presently *absent* one who is to return.[13] For Paul, therefore, the community's eucharistic remembrance is compounded of participation in the life-giving death of its Lord and anticipation of his coming.

Some interpreters maintain that "until" (*achri hou*) has not only durative force, referring to the passing of time, but also telic force, "*so that* he may come."[14] Whatever the case, Paul's reference to the Lord's coming is one more expression of the eschatological expectation that surfaces repeatedly in this letter, from the opening thanksgiving (1.7–8) to its closing lines (16.22, "Our Lord, come!"). By writing of the Lord's return and God's final victory the apostle is putting a brake on the Corinthians' excessive claims about possessing religious wisdom and experiencing the riches of salvation (e.g., 1.4–8; 8.2; 13.9–12); and no less, he is reminding them of who it is to whom they are ultimately accountable (e.g., 3.10–4.5).

Ultimate accountability is an explicit consideration as Paul urges his congregation to change its practices at the Lord's supper: "[W]hoever eats the bread or drinks the cup of the Lord inappropriately will be liable for the body and blood of the Lord" (v. 27). In the case at hand, what he means by "inappropriately" (*anaxiōs*) is evident when he expresses his displeasure with the disorder and inequities of the Corinthian celebration (vv. 18, 20–21), and as he goes on to warn about "[not] discerning the body" (v. 29). When the Corinthians fail to manifest the love by which they have been graced and formed into a community of faith through Jesus' life-giving death, they are violating the body of the Lord himself, who is present in and with the gifts of bread and wine.

Paul is arguing here exactly as he had when the issue was

---

[13] Cf. Klauck, "Presence in the Lord's Supper," 69.

[14] E.g., Otfried Hofius, "'Bis daß er kommt': I Kor. xii.26," *NTS* 14 (1968), 439–41, and "The Lord's Supper," 111–12.

whether to eat meat from pagan sacrifices, if doing so would put at risk the "weak" in faith for whom such meat was taboo: to sin against others is to sin against Christ, whose life-giving death for others establishes their identity as a community of brothers and sisters bound together by the gift and claim of his love (8.11–12). Indeed, already in this earlier context Paul has commented on what it means for the community to gather at the table where their Lord is the host. In the course of expanding his counsels about temple meat to include a warning about idolatry (10.1–22), he combines the traditional identification of the eucharistic bread as Christ's "body" (*sōma*) with his own understanding of what it means to be called into Christ's "company" (*koinōnia*); and in the process, the meaning of each term is broadened: "The bread that we break, is it not a sharing (*koinōnia*) in Christ's body? Because there is one bread, we who are many are one body, for we all partake of the one bread" (10.16b–17).

In the first statement, which draws on the tradition, the eucharistic loaf is associated with the body of the crucified Christ, in *koinōnia* with whom the community has its life (see 1.9b). In the second statement the community is being thought of as a body – indeed "*one* body" whose unity like its life derives from participation in Christ's death. Along with his example of the Israelites in the wilderness who had been "cut down" for their idolatry (vv. 1–13), Paul's affirmation of this twofold *koinōnia* that is nourished at the Lord's table – a *koinōnia* both with the host and with one another – supports his appeal to flee from idolatry (v. 14). He means that those who belong to the Lord must not eat in pagan temples (cf. 8.10) where sacrifices are offered to "demons" (evidently the "so-called" gods and lords mentioned in 8.5), because those who gather at their table become partners (*koinōnoi*) with them (v. 20). For Paul, because the Lord's claim is total and excludes all other claims, there can be no sharing in the table of demons without abandoning the table where the Lord is host and true life is present (v. 21). Again here, we are in touch with one of the most pervasive and decisive themes in 1 Corinthians: belonging to Christ means belonging to God (3.23), by whom all things are given and all things are claimed (8.6).

Clearly, Paul's view of the eucharistic bread as representing not only the crucified body of Christ (10.16) but also the "one body" of those who are incorporated into his life-giving death (10.17), has informed his subsequent criticisms of how the Lord's supper is typically observed in the Corinthian church (11.17–34). The evidence he presents for the Corinthians not actually observing the *Lord's* supper is their manifest lack of concern for one another when they are assembled for that purpose (vv. 18–21). Moreover, when he warns them about not "discerning the body" (v. 29), the term *sōma* likely carries both of the meanings it has in chapter 10: what is to be discerned in the bread of the Lord's supper is both "Christ's body" given for others and that the "many" for whom Christ died are "one body" in him.

THE BELIEVING COMMUNITY

The most important aspects of Paul's thinking about the church have emerged in connection with his call for congregational unity (chapters 1–4), and these are simply presupposed throughout the remainder of the letter. Even in chapters 12–14, where he has special reason to reflect further on life in the believing community and where he effectively compares it with a human body (12.12–30), he is only elaborating and illustrating motifs that have been present all along.

As we have seen, the prescript provides Paul's correspondents with two key elements for their self-understanding as a congregation: they are "*God's* church in Corinth," and they have been called of God to be "*holy* people" who are "*sanctified* in Christ Jesus" (1.2). In the thanksgiving they are further described as recipients of God's grace (1.4–7a) and as "called into the company of his Son, Jesus Christ our Lord" (1.9). This view of the church as God's people set apart for God's service, which was influenced, clearly, by Paul's Jewish heritage, is also evident in three images he employs in chapter 3. There he portrays the church as "God's field," in which the seeds of the gospel have been sown (3.9), "God's building" (*oikodomē*), which is founded on Jesus Christ and built up through the labors of God's ministers (3.9, 10–15), and "God's temple," which is indwelt by God's Holy Spirit (3.16–17).

Paul's image of the church as God's temple is not an extension of the building imagery, which included concern for the builders and their ultimate accountability to God. In the temple image attention is centered on the sanctifying presence of the indwelling Spirit of God, and the sure destruction that will be visited upon anyone who violates the temple's holiness. Concern for the sanctity of the believing community is especially apparent in the counsels of chapters 5 and 6 about dealing with an errant member of the congregation and avoiding litigation in pagan courts. This portrayal of the community as God's holy temple corresponds both with Paul's characterization of his *congregation* in the prescript and with his subsequent identification of the *individual* believer as "a temple of the indwelling Holy Spirit" (6.19). In their belonging individually to God, believers belong as well to the whole people of God.

As we have also seen, Paul's counsels and argument in the first eleven chapters reflect his view that the church, by reason of its divine calling, exists as a community of the end-time. To be sure, he regards the church as situated in the present age and necessarily involved with it (e.g., 2.7; 5.10), and he emphasizes that its members receive God's call and are summoned to live as befits this call in their present social circumstances (7.17–24). Yet he also understands the church to derive its life and mission from the age to come, the saving power of which is already operative in God's electing love (8.1–3; cf. 10.11) as this is demonstrated in the cross (1.18–2.16; cf. 8.11). Moreover, because the believing community has been founded and formed by the saving power of God's love, believers fulfill their calling to belong to God as they commit themselves, both corporately and individually, to be agents of God's love in the world. Looking back, one can see that this understanding has informed the apostle's call for unity (e.g., 1.10; 4.6), his advice about disputes with fellow believers (6.7–8), his counsels to do nothing to injure those who lack the knowledge that comes with faith (8.1–11.1), and his call to celebrate the Lord's supper in a way that is appropriate to the significance of the Lord's death (11.17–34).

All of these themes are at work in chapters 12–14, where the apostle is concerned to moderate his congregation's lofty estimate of spiritual gifts, especially glossolalia (speaking in tongues).[15] After providing several specific directives for the conduct of its worship (14.26–36), he ends up with a very general, summary appeal, to "let everything be done properly and with order" (14.40). There is nothing distinctively Christian about this rule; parallels may be found in a number of other ancient texts, both Jewish and pagan, which are concerned with the ordering of cultic assemblies.[16] However, this otherwise commonplace directive takes on a more distinctly Pauline meaning when it is read in the context provided by the other counsels and the overall argument in chapters 12–14. In particular, this call for propriety and good order has to be interpreted in connection with the similarly formulated and functionally parallel appeal in 14.26c, "Let everything be done for building up." Together, these two appeals supply the framework within which the more specific instructions are presented. However, it is the first one that gathers up the discussion since 12.1 and thereby represents Paul's real concern. The end that he has in view is not just decorum in the assembly but the upbuilding of the church in love (14.1–5, 12, 17).

The appeals and directives of chapter 14 are founded on two premises, although they are not stated as premises, which are apparent in the introductory paragraphs of Paul's discussion of spiritual gifts (12.1–11). First, because "no one can say, 'Jesus is Lord,' except by the Holy Spirit" (v. 3), all believers are beneficiaries of the Spirit's working. For the apostle, it follows from this that every believer has received some spiritual gift, that the gifts

---

[15] For important, representative studies of Paul's view of the church which include attention to these chapters, see, e.g., James D. G. Dunn, "'The Body of Christ' in Paul," *Worship, Theology and Ministry in the Early Church: Essays in Honor of Ralph P. Martin*, JSNTSup 87 (ed. by M. Wilkins and T. Paige; Sheffield, 1992), 146–62; Wolfgang Kraus, *Das Volk Gottes. Zur Grundlegung der Ekklesiologie bei Paulus*, WUNT 2/85 (Tübingen, 1996); Andreas Lindemann, "Die Kirche als Leib. Beobachtungen zur 'demokratischen' Ekklesiologie bei Paulus," *ZTK* 92 (1995), 140–65; D. B. Martin, *Corinthian Body*, esp. 87–103; Ralph P. Martin, *The Spirit and the Congregation. Studies in I Corinthians 12–15* (Grand Rapids, 1984); Helmut Merklein, "Entstehung und Gehalt des paulinischen Leib-Christi-Gedankens," *Studien zu Jesus und Paulus*, WUNT 2/43 (Tübingen, 1987), 319–44; Thomas Söding, "'Ihr aber seid der Leib Christi' (1 Kor 12, 27). Exegetische Beobachtungen an einem zentralen Motiv paulinischer Ekklesiologie," *Catholica* 45 (1991), 135–62.

[16] Examples in Gerhard Dautzenberg, *Urchristliche Prophetie. Ihre Erforschung ihre Voraussetzungen im Judentum und ihre Struktur im ersten Korintherbrief*, BWANT 104 (Stuttgart, 1975), 279.

are of many different types, and that all have been provided "by one and the same Spirit" (vv. 4–6, 8–11). Second, these varied gifts of the Spirit, although individually bestowed, have been given "for the benefit of all" (v. 7, *pros to sympheron*). Both of these premises are critical for Paul's argument. The first invalidates any attempt to rank believers according to the kind of spiritual gift they have, and the second introduces a criterion for governing how spiritual gifts are to be employed. As the course of his discussion will show, Paul means that spiritual gifts are not to be used to enhance one's standing in the congregation, but "for building up" (*pros oikodomēn*) the church as a whole (14.26c; cf. the parallel statements in 10.23: "not everything is beneficial [*sympherei*] . . . not everything builds up [*oikodomei*]").

The two-part excursus which constitutes the remainder of chapters 12–13 supports and expands on these two premises. In the first part, the apostle argues that the diversity of spiritual gifts both manifests and serves the unity that is given with life in Christ (12.12–30). In the second part, and in keeping with his dictum that "knowledge inflates, but love builds up" (8.1b), he indicates by what measure and means the spiritual gifts are to be evaluated and employed for the community's benefit (12.31–13.13).

Many members, one body

In the first part of the excursus Paul likens the community of believers to a human body, which has various "members" but remains an organic whole. This metaphor appears often in the literature of Greek and Roman antiquity, variously applied (especially to political matters), and may well have been familiar to the apostle's Corinthian correspondents.[17] As employed by Paul, it is meant to support the view that those who belong to Christ (confessing him as "Lord," v. 3) have been baptized into "one body" with a richly diverse membership, and that by enabling the body

---

[17] Lindemann ("Die Kirche als Leib," 143–46) identifies four principal ways the metaphor was applied, referring to passages in the works of Plato, Aristotle, Cicero, Livy (who cites Menenius Agrippa), Seneca, Epictetus, and others. See also M. Eugene Boring, Klaus Berger, and Carsten Colpe, *Hellenistic Commentary to the New Testament* (Nashville, 1995), nos. 694–96.

to function properly this diversity actually serves its unity (vv. 12–17).[18]

In itself, the judgment that diversity may serve the cause of unity is a matter of political philosophy, not religious conviction.[19] Paul, however, proceeds to undergird the point theologically: "But in fact, God placed the members in the body, each and every one of them, just as he chose" (v. 18). This corresponds to his earlier comment that the varied gifts are distributed "to each person individually, just as the Spirit chooses" (v. 11), and it is echoed in his subsequent remark about the divine intentionality that is evident in the way the body works (v. 24; see also v. 28). Moreover, this theological affirmation prompts him to a further and strengthened exposition of his point that diversity is necessary for the healthy functioning of the body (vv. 19–26). Now, perhaps specifically with the Corinthian congregation in mind, he claims that even its weaker, dishonorable, and unpresentable parts are indispensable (vv. 22–24a); indeed, that "God has so composed the body as to give the neediest the greater honor," in order that the members of the body might be united in their caring for one another, in their suffering, and in their rejoicing (vv. 25b–26).

In vv. 27–30 the apostle's focus remains on the diversity that characterizes the oneness of the congregation. Since believers are "individually members" of Christ,[20] they manifest different gifts and have been appointed to different roles within the church. In his introductory statement, "Now you are the body of Christ" (v. 27), Paul is neither presupposing nor introducing a doctrine of the church as "the body of Christ," but simply asking his congregation

[18] The point that Paul is emphasizing diversity no less than oneness is apt to be lost when v. 14 ("For indeed, the body is not one member but many") is separated from the preceding verses and taken as the beginning of a new paragraph. In my view, a new paragraph is not clearly signaled until v. 18, where *nuni de* ("But in fact, . . .") introduces a theological point (see below).

[19] See, e.g., Plato, *Republic* 5.462d (Boring, Berger, Colpe, *Hellenistic Commentary*, no. 696, with comments); Aristotle, *Politics* 5.1302b.33–40.

[20] The expression, *melē ek merous* (v. 27), is usually paraphrased as "individually members *of it*," assuming a reference to the word "body." But the Greek allows and the context recommends construing the phrase with "Christ," yielding: "But you are the body of Christ, and individually members *of him*." This interpretation is supported by 6.15, where, for emphasis, Paul twice identifies believers (*their* "bodies") as "members of Christ" (*melē [tou] Christou*).

to think of itself as a "body" that belongs to Christ.[21] Later writers will elaborate this metaphor by identifying Christ as "the head of the body, the church" (Col. 1.18; cf. 2.19; Eph. 4.15–16; 5.23), but it is significant that Paul himself does not take this step (in v. 21 he has mentioned "the head" as simply one member like all of the others). For him, believers are "in Christ," not simply "under" him, because Christ's lordship is not defined by power alone, as in the case of earthly sovereigns, but by the saving power of God's love as revealed in the cross.

From the way Paul introduces the body metaphor, it is evident that he associates both baptism and the working of the Spirit with one's incorporation into the believing community: "For indeed, in the one Spirit we were all baptized into one body – whether Jews or Greeks, whether slaves or free – and we were all made to drink of one Spirit" (v. 13). Although there is no further mention in this excursus of either baptism or the Spirit, each has a significant place in Paul's thinking about the church. Before we move on to the second part of the excursus, therefore, it is worth pausing to consider what views about baptism and the Holy Spirit are reflected in 1 Corinthians overall.

Baptism

There are four places in 1 Corinthians where Paul mentions baptism, more than in any of his other letters, yet baptism itself is never his principal topic. He seems to assume that the Corinthians have a generally adequate understanding of the significance of this rite, even when he expresses relief that he did not baptize many of them, because that could have encouraged the partisan spirit he decries (1.13–17). Elsewhere in the letter Paul remarks that the Israelites had been "baptized into Moses" (10.1–2), that believers have been "baptized into one body" (12.13), and that his Corinthian congregation practices "baptism on behalf of the dead" (15.29, NRSV). The latter, enigmatic reference, no matter how it is to be construed, discloses nothing about the apostle's own

---

[21] See, esp., Lindemann, "Die Kirche als Leib," 152. Similarly, Dunn, who suggests that "*the Christ-relatedness of the body*" (his emphasis) is constitutive for the "body of Christ" theme, which Paul does not state with "dogmatic precision" but with "metaphorical imprecision" ("'The Body of Christ,'" 150, 151).

understanding of baptism.[22] However, the three remaining passages offer at least some clues, as does a statement in 6.11 ("but you
were washed," etc.) which draws on baptismal language. Although
these clues do not add up to a "doctrine" of baptism, even one
geared to the argument of 1 Corinthians, they do put us in touch
with several aspects of the apostle's thinking about this Christian
rite, at least as it surfaces in this particular letter.

First, a series of rhetorical questions with which Paul challenges
his congregation to manifest the unity they have been given in
Christ suggests that he associates baptism closely with one's appro-
priating the benefits of Christ's saving death. "Christ isn't divided,
is he? Paul wasn't crucified for you, was he? You weren't baptized
'in the name of Paul,' were you?" (1.13) The second and third questions, which are closely linked by the references to Paul, allude,
respectively, to Christ's crucifixion and to baptism in the name of
Christ (cf. 6.11). Here there is at least a hint of the view the apostle
will express later on, in Romans, that baptism "into Christ Jesus"
is baptism "into his death" (Rom. 6.3–4).

Second, for Paul, baptism into Christ means, simultaneously,
incorporation into a community of believers who, in their belonging to him, are many and yet one. As we have seen, he introduces
the body metaphor in order to make exactly this point (12.12–13).
Although baptism distinguishes believers from nonbelievers, it
does not distinguish one believer from another ("we were *all* baptized into one body"). Rather, baptism initiates believers into a
community where they gain a new and shared identity in Christ,
even while retaining their individuality (e.g., as "Jews or
Greeks . . . slaves or free"). The rhetorical questions in 1.13 reflect
this same conviction: because "Christ isn't divided" there is no
place for divisions among those who have been baptized in the
name of the one who was crucified for them.

Third, Paul understands baptism to involve one's deliverance
from an old way of life and transfer into the sphere where Christ
is Lord. This, too, is hinted at in chapter 1, where the apostle's challenging questions are directed to those who profess commitment to

22   In addition to the commentaries, see Joel R. White, " 'Baptized on account of the Dead':
     The Meaning of 1 Corinthians 15:29 in Its Context," *JBL* 116 (1997), 487–99.

some particular leader like himself or Apollos (vv. 11–12). Because it is in *Christ's* name and into *his* death that they have been baptized, they now belong to *him alone*. The same is suggested when Paul describes Israel's relationship to Moses on the analogy of baptism into Christ – the Israelites were "baptized into Moses in the cloud and in the sea . . ." (10.2, NRSV). Baptism means liberation from slavery into the new life that is given with belonging to Christ (cf. 7.22). The declaration of 6.11, formulated in the language of the church's baptismal traditions, corresponds with this. In contrast with what they once were (cf. vv. 9–10), believers have been "washed, . . . sanctified, . . . rectified 'in the name of the Lord Jesus Christ' and in the Spirit of our God" (cf. 1.30).

Fourth, it is evident that Paul associates baptism closely with the reception and empowering presence of the Spirit. When he affirms that "in the one Spirit" (12.13; cf. 6.11) all believers have been "baptized into one body," he appears to identify the Spirit as both instrumental to the deliverance that baptism represents and the sphere within which that deliverance occurs. His further comment that believers "were all made to drink of one Spirit" (12.13, NRSV) provides a vivid image of the Spirit's pervasive and enlivening presence within the community of the baptized.[23]

Finally, however much the apostle may have regarded baptism as signifying, confirming, or even actualizing one's transfer from death's domain to the realm where Christ is Lord, nothing in 1 Corinthians suggests that he viewed baptism itself as *effecting* this transfer. To be sure, every time he mentions baptism in this letter he assumes its significance. And his claim that Christ did not send him to baptize but to preach the gospel (1.17) – although he admits to having baptized an indeterminate number of people in Corinth (1.14–16) – by no means constitutes a negative estimate of the rite. Nonetheless, his conviction that the "foundation" of Jesus Christ on which the believing community is built (3.10–11) is laid only through the preaching of the cross (e.g., 1.18–2.16), which is his own

---

[23] It is conceivable, but no more, that Paul is alluding to the Spirit's role in baptism when he remarks that the Israelites "were baptized into Moses *in the cloud*" (which had guided them by day, Exod. 13.21–22; cf. Ps. 105.39; Wisd. 19.7–8) as well as "in the sea" (10.2). Cf. Schrage, *Der erste Brief*, II, 392, who notes the references in vv. 3–4 to Israel's "spiritual" food and drink.

particular calling (2.2; 9.16), would seem to preclude any notion of baptism as either *mediating* God's saving power or *initiating* one's believing acceptance of the gospel. Indeed, he warns the Corinthians not to repeat the folly of Israel in the wilderness by supposing that their baptism (or their participation in the Lord's supper) guarantees them salvation (10.1–4).

The Spirit

Paul mentions the Spirit quite often in 1 Corinthians, no doubt prompted by his concern to correct extravagant and divisive claims that some were making about their possession of spiritual gifts. Accordingly, most of his references to the Spirit occur in chapters 12 and 14, although there is a smaller but equally important concentration of comments about the Spirit in chapter 2. The apostle ordinarily refers simply to "the Spirit," but occasionally he is explicit about its being the Spirit of (or "from") God (2.11, 12, 14; 3.16; 6.11; 7.40; 12.3), and in two places he describes it as the "holy" Spirit (6.19; 12.3; cf. 3.17).[24] It is too much to claim that, for Paul, "the Spirit is the key to everything,"[25] even if one applies this judgment only to 1 Corinthians. There is no doubt, however, that in this letter Paul attaches considerable importance to the working of the Spirit in two major respects.

First, and decisively, he associates the Spirit with the *founding* and *initial formation* of a believing community. He says that his missionary preaching in Corinth – of Jesus Christ crucified (2.2) – was "with a demonstration of the Spirit and of power" (2.4, NRSV), and that through the Spirit's working one is able to receive the secret "wisdom" of the cross as the revelation of the saving purposes and power of God (2.6–10). Paul expands on this role of the Spirit in mediating the knowledge of God by drawing an analogy with one's knowledge of other people. Just as no one understands a person's innermost being "except the human spirit within [that] person," so "no one has understood what is truly God's except the Spirit of God" (2.11). Therefore, he concludes (perhaps alluding to baptism), "[w]e did not receive the spirit of the world but the Spirit

---

[24] For detailed comments on all of the occurrences in 1 Corinthians, see (in addition to the standard commentaries) Fee, *God's Empowering Presence*, 81–281.   [25] Ibid., 83, 98, 105.

that is from God, in order that we may understand what has been graciously bestowed on us by God" (2.12). Here one sees the conceptual underpinning of Paul's later claim that "no one can say, 'Jesus is Lord,' except by the Holy Spirit" (12.3).

The Spirit is also associated with conversion in the declaration that believers have been washed, sanctified, and rectified "in the Spirit of our God" as well as " 'in the name of the Lord Jesus Christ' " (6.11). Although Paul may connect the Spirit's work particularly with sanctification, which sets believers apart as God's holy people and for the service of God, he does not actually make that connection here. He does make it, however, when, in support of his claim that one's whole being belongs to the Lord (6.13), he identifies the body of the individual believer as "a temple of the indwelling Holy Spirit" (6.19); and again, when he calls on his congregation – a *community* of believers – to understand itself as "God's temple," made holy by God's presence through the Spirit (3.16–17). These two modes of the Spirit's sanctifying presence, with the individual and with the community, come together when Paul highlights the Spirit's role in forming the "many" baptized into "one body" in Christ (12.13). The Spirit is thus instrumental in establishing the wholeness as well as the holiness of the believing community.

A second, closely related aspect of the Spirit's role, as Paul writes of it in 1 Corinthians, is the continual *upbuilding* of this believing community. It is to this end, he believes, that the Spirit has chosen to grace believers individually with varied gifts (12.4–11) – that the body and all of its members might function as God intends. What God intends, according to Paul, is "the benefit of all" (12.7), which comes about as the gifts that are "energized" by the Spirit (12.11) are then exercised in love (14.1–5; cf. 12.31–13.13). Consistent with this, he believes that the Spirit attends his own work as an apostle (7.40; cf. 12.28, 29), informing the words that he speaks for the congregation's upbuilding in love (2.13; cf. 4.21).

Despite the importance that Paul attaches to the working of the Spirit, both in his ministry and in the believing community overall, there is no considered doctrine of the Spirit in 1 Corinthians. There is also nothing in this letter to suggest that he has reflected on precisely how the Spirit or the Spirit's working is related to God and Christ. For example, when he mentions Christ and the Spirit as together constituting the source and sphere of the believers' new life (6.11) he shows no concern to distinguish their respective roles. Nor do his successive references in 12.4, 5, 6 to "the same Spirit," "the same Lord," and "the same God" have any special doctrinal significance. Rather, these serve the rhetorical purpose of emphasizing that the varied gifts have *one and the same* divine source. This passage provides no grounds for describing the apostle's views as even implicitly "trinitarian." For example, he seems not to have considered how the functions of the Spirit may differ from the functions of God. While he initially identifies *God* as the one who activates the various gifts (12.5), he subsequently identifies *the Spirit* as doing so (12.11). Similarly, he follows up his comment that the distribution of gifts to the members of the body is a matter of *the Spirit's* choosing (12.11) with a generally parallel statement that "*God* placed the members in the body, each and every one of them, just as he chose" (12.18).[26]

Indeed, the apostle's *two-part* affirmation of "one God" and "one Lord" (8.6; cf. the two-part formulation in 1.3) is much more representative of the understanding of God that is characteristic of this letter; namely, that the crucified Christ is the definitive revelation of God's saving power (1.18–2.5), and that belonging to Christ means belonging also to God (3.23). As we have seen, the Spirit, which Paul associates with "the very depths of God," is identified as the medium of God's self-disclosure in Christ and indispensable for receiving that revelation (2.10–15). However, the Spirit is not identified as either the source of revelation or the revealer per se.[27]

The "most excellent way"

The theological foundation for chapter 14 continues to be laid in the second part of the excursus (12.31–13.13). To be sure, the finely-

---

[26] Contrast Fee, *First Epistle*, 588, and *God's Empowering Presence*, 162–63.

[27] Paul's comment that Christ, the eschatological Adam, was "a life-giving spirit" (15.45) offers no help in understanding how the apostle may have construed the relationship of Christ and the Spirit. In the context where this statement occurs his topic is *Adam* and Christ, and the "spiritual body" with which the dead shall be raised. Cf. Fee, *God's Empowering Presence*, 264–67; James D. G. Dunn, *The Theology of Paul the Apostle* (Grand Rapids, 1998), 260–64; and see below, 114.

crafted rhetoric and elevated style of chapter 13 have led to various proposals about its origin and, therefore, its relation to the present context. Was it written for another occasion, perhaps even by someone other than Paul, and then taken over by the apostle because he thought it could help him make a point about spiritual gifts? Most interpreters judge it to be Paul's composition, and acknowledge its appropriateness for this context even if it was already at hand when he began to dictate the letter.[28] Whatever the particular rhetorical genre to which it bears the closest resemblance (it exhibits characteristics of several, including the encomium, demonstrative discourse, and deliberative discourse[29]), its function within the argument of chapters 12–14 is quite clear. Supplementing the metaphor of the body, it helps to prepare for the appeals and instructions which follow (chapter 14) by emphasizing that every spiritual gift is incomplete and of only passing significance, and that the one enduring reality, apart from which humanity cannot flourish, is love (*agapē*).

To an introductory appeal, "Be eager for the greater gifts [*ta charismata ta meizona*]" (12.31a), Paul immediately adds, "and I am going to show you the most excellent way" (12.31b). Read without reference to the overall context, the appeal seems to contradict his own claim that all gifts have the same divine source and are equally important for the functioning of the body. Read in context, however, it comes across as an ironic appeal. It is apparent that believers in Corinth are already eager for "the greater gifts," by which they mean the more spectacular and personally enhancing. But Paul's exposition of "the most excellent way" effectively shifts attention away from what gifts may be "greater" to the matter of

---

[28] In addition to the commentaries, see the studies cited above, chapter 1, nn. 21, 22, and in n. 32 below (also Mitchell, *Paul and the Rhetoric of Reconciliation*, 270–71).

[29] As an encomium, e.g., George A. Kennedy, *New Testament Interpretation through Rhetorical Criticism* (Chapel Hill and London, 1984), 18, 156, and James G. Sigountos, "The Genre of 1 Corinthians 13," *NTS* 40 (1994), 246–60; as demonstrative rhetoric, e.g., Joop F. M. Smit, "The Genre of 1 Corinthians 13 in the Light of Classical Rhetoric," *NovT* 33 (1991), 193–216, and Jan Lambrecht, "The Most Eminent Way. A Study of 1 Corinthians 13," *Pauline Studies. Collected Essays*, BETL 115 (Leuven, 1994), 79–107, here: 87; as an "exemplary argument" set within the overall deliberative rhetoric of the letter, e.g., Mitchell, *Paul and the Rhetoric of Reconciliation*, 270–29. Oda Wischmeyer, *Der höchste Weg. Das 13. Kapitel des 1. Korintherbriefes*, SNT 13 (Gütersloh, 1981), 217–23, describes it more generally as "a religious-ethical discourse."

what benefits the whole community (12.7) by building it up. At the same time, it subordinates all spiritual gifts to the one abiding reality of *agapē*, and warrants his *replacing* the initial, ironic appeal with new and utterly serious ones: "Pursue love, and [then you can!] be eager for the spiritual gifts [*ta pneumatika*] – but most especially that you may prophesy" (14.1); and "Since you are [already!] eager for spiritual gifts [*pneumatōn*], try to excel in building up the church" (14.12).[30]

There is nothing explicitly theological about chapter 13, which yields not a single reference to God, Christ, or the Spirit, and where glossolalia, prophecy, and knowledge, although mentioned, are never identified as either divine gifts (*charismata*) or spiritual phenomena (*pneumatika*). When one looks more closely, however, it becomes apparent that Paul's exposition of *agapē* proceeds from the theological premise about knowledge and love which he set forth in 8.1–3, and which informs much of this letter. As we have seen, in the context of his counsels about eating meat from pagan temples this premise supports several key points: that one's relationship to God is founded not on human attempts to know God but on God's prior electing grace, to which one's love of God is a believing response; that knowing and believing in "one God, the Father" means, no less, knowing and believing in "one Lord, Jesus Christ" who died for all (8.6, 11); and that when the beneficiaries of God's love fail to be agents of that love (for instance, in relation to those who are weak in faith), they sin against Christ himself (8.12). It is this love, by which one is graced and claimed ("known"), that is the saving power of God revealed in the cross, and because it is constitutive of the new creation it is an *eschatological* power.[31] This, primarily, is the *agapē* Paul is writing about in chapter 13: *God's love manifested in Christ, which is the eschatological power of God for salvation.*[32]

[30] For other arguments in favor of taking the appeal of 12.31a as ironic, see Joop F. M. Smit, "Two Puzzles: 1 Corinthians 12.31 and 13.3: A Rhetorical Solution," *NTS* 39 (1993), 246–64, here: 247–53. In view of the reformulations in 14.1, 12, which are certainly imperatives, 12.31a should probably not be read as a rhetorical question (thus, e.g., Martin, *The Spirit and the Congregation*, 35), although doing so results in an interpretation very close to the one offered here.   [31] See above, 72–75.

[32] The theological character of this chapter has been demonstrated in a number of studies, including: Günther Bornkamm, "The More Excellent Way (I Corinthians 13)," *Early*

Working from his premise about love and knowledge, Paul further prepares for the appeals and instructions of chapter 14 by emphasizing the necessity of love (vv. 1–3), its work (vv. 4–7), and its permanence (vv. 8–13).

The necessity of love

No matter how marvelous one's gifts and capacities, apart from *agapē* one is "nothing" (v. 2). And no matter how much one gives up, apart from *agapē* one has gained no advantage (v. 3).[33] As regards the issue at hand, these statements shift attention away from the spiritual gifts themselves to what must accompany them, and thus to the purpose for which they are bestowed. That purpose, Paul has said, is to benefit all (12.7), not to enhance one's own status within the community.

In this context, and consistent with the parallel expressions in 10.23, "not everything is beneficial . . . not everything builds up," what benefits all is the upbuilding of the church. One's gifts are to be employed in accord with what love requires and as love directs, because love is what "builds up" (8.1b); and as Paul has shown earlier (8.7–12), what love requires and directs is to be determined with reference to *God's* love disclosed in the cross.

Beyond their pertinence for the matter of spiritual gifts, these statements amount to an affirmation that *agapē* is essential for human flourishing, and therefore definitive of human existence itself, even as it is definitive of God and constitutive of God's

---

Christian Experience, 180–93; Kurt Niederwimmer, "Erkennen und Lieben. Gedanken zum Verhältnis von Gnosis und Agape im ersten Korintherbrief," *KD* 11 (1965), 75–102; Sigfred Pedersen, "Agape – der eschatologische Hauptbegriff bei Paulus," *Die Paulinische Literatur und Theologie. The Pauline Literature and Theology* (ed. by S. Pedersen; Åarhus and Göttingen, 1980), 159–86; Wischmeyer, *Der höchste Weg*, esp. 92–116; Benoît Standaert, "1 Corinthiens 13," *Charisma und Agape (1Co 12–14)*, Benedictina, Biblical-ecumenical section, 7 (ed. by Lorenzo de Lorenzi; Rome, 1983), 127–39 (with discussion, 139–47); D. A. Carson, *Showing the Spirit: A Theological Exposition of 1 Corinthians 12–14* (Grand Rapids, 1987), 51–76; Carl R. Holladay, "1 Corinthians 13: Paul as Apostolic Paradigm," *Greeks, Romans, and Christians*, 80–98; Lambrecht, "The Most Eminent Way"; Söding, *Liebesgebot*, 124–49; Romano Penna, "Only Love Will Have No End. A Reading of 1 Corinthians 13 in Its Various Senses," *Paul the Apostle* (Collegeville, 1996), I.191–205.

33 Whether Paul spoke of handing over his body "so that I may boast" (NRSV, translating *hina kauchēsōmai*) or "to be burned" (NRSVmg., translating *hina kauthēsōmai*) does not affect the main point: no matter how much one may give up, nothing has been gained if love is lacking.

electing grace and saving power. Here, already, the theological orientation of the chapter is clear, because for Paul, at least, one is always either "something" or "nothing" only in relation to God (e.g., 1.26–31; 3.7).[34]

The work of love

In verses 4–7 Paul moves on, not to describe the intrinsic "nature" of *agapē*, but to indicate how love manifests itself concretely in history. It is not impossible that the apostle wants his congregation to identify his ministry in Corinth with how love acts, and its own conduct with what love avoids.[35] However, the more fundamental point is that by personifying love, as he has in these verses, Paul represents it as a reality – not inert, but constantly active – that is independent of any human disposition, attitude, or feeling.

This is, in fact, the reality of God's own gracious, saving activity, as that is represented in numerous scriptural passages, doubtless well known to Paul, where God is affirmed as forbearing and kind (v. 4; cf. Rom. 2.4; 9.22; 11.22),[36] not abiding wickedness (v. 6a; cf. Rom.1.29; 2.8),[37] but also not tallying up evil (v. 5e; cf. 2 Cor. 5.19; Rom. 4.7–8).[38] This is also the reality of God as manifested definitively in the crucified Christ, who did not seek his own advantage (v. 5b; cf. Rom. 15.1–6; Phil. 2.4, 6) but gave himself for others. Accordingly, when Paul appeals to the Corinthians to imitate him as he imitates Christ (11.1), he is summoning them to be agents of this divine *agapē*, a love that sets aside self-interest in order to work for the benefit of others (thus 10.24, 33).

The permanence of love

The concluding paragraph of the excursus is framed by the statements of vv. 8a ("Love never ends") and 13a ("Thus faith, hope,

---

[34] Cf. Söding, *Liebesgebot*, 130.   [35] Thus Holladay, "1 Corinthians 13," 94–97.

[36] See Thomas Söding, *Die Trias Glaube, Hoffnung, Liebe bei Paulus. Eine exegetische Studie*, SBS 150 (Stuttgart, 1992), 123 and nn. 57, 58, who cites, e.g., Exod. 34.6–7; Num. 14.18; Pss. 24[25].6–10; 30.20 [31.19]; 33.9 [34.8]; 67.11 [68.10]; 84.13 [85.12]; 85[86].5, 15; 102[103].8; Jonah 4.2; Wisd. 15.1.

[37] E.g., Pss. 11.6; 66.18; 92.15; Judith 5.17.

[38] See, esp., Ps. 32.2, which Paul himself is citing in Rom. 4.7–8; Söding, *Die Trias*, 123, n. 59.

and love remain, these three"), which thereby provide its theme, the enduring reality of love. This may be hinted at already in v. 7, if the fourfold "all things" (*panta*) not only identifies what love endures, believes, hopes, and perseveres in, but also has an adverbial aspect ("always").[39] But now Paul specifically emphasizes love's continuing reality, contrasting this with the temporary and imperfect character of spiritual gifts (vv. 8b–9). Even the most beneficial of those gifts, like prophesying, belong to this present, passing age (cf. 7.29–31) and participate in its imperfection. For Paul, it is not just a matter of the temporary imperfection or incompleteness of the gifts. He speaks not of their one day being perfected or completed, but of their coming to an end (*katargēthēsetai*, vv. 8b–10), and his illustration of this leaves no doubt about his point: "When I was a child I talked like a child, thought like a child, reasoned like a child; when I became a man I put an end to childhood ways [*katērgēka ta tou nēpiou*]" (v. 11). Clearly, the apostle wants his audience to infer from this that love belongs to an order of reality that does not end, and thus manifests the perfection (*to teleion*) of what is to come.

The line of thought developed in verses 8b–10 is extended in verse 12, but in the process Paul both narrows and enlarges his discussion. He narrows it, because just as he had mentioned glossolalia along with prophesying and knowledge in verse 8, but then not in verse 9, he now leaves prophesying, too, behind to focus exclusively on knowledge. He also enlarges his discussion, however, by shifting attention to another kind of knowledge. His subject is no longer the special gift of knowledge granted by the Spirit to some and not to others, but the knowledge that is constitutive of one's relationship to God. This shift of meaning begins with his use of a metaphor which contrasts the indirect and therefore partial vision provided by a mirror with the kind of seeing that is direct and complete: "For now we see in a mirror, indirectly, but then face to face" (v. 12a). Although the distinction made here between "now" and "then" is roughly analogous to the one in verse 11 between childhood and adulthood, this statement moves beyond the preceding one by bringing to the surface the

---

[39] Thus Lambrecht, "The Most Eminent Way," 91.

underlying eschatological orientation of this whole chapter. "Now," in this present age, one sees only indirectly and imperfectly; but "then," in the age to come, one will see "face to face."[40]

The point of this metaphor is given in the second part of the verse, where Paul speaks again of knowledge: "Now I know in part [*ginōskō ek merous*], but then I will know fully even as I have been fully known [*tote de epignōsomai kathōs kai epegnōsthēn*]" (v. 12b). It is clear from both the context, which affirms the enduring reality and critical importance of love, and the reference to knowing as one has "been known," that the underlying premise is the one Paul has set forth in 8.1–3 about knowledge and love. However extensive and significant one's knowledge about God, because it belongs only to this age it remains indirect, as in a mirror, and therefore partial. But Paul anticipates that in the age to come one's knowledge of God will be of a radically different order, a direct, "face to face" communion with God that is appropriate to the saving power of *agapē* by which one has already "been known" (graced and claimed) by God (*kathōs kai epegnōsthēn*; cf. 8.3, "known by him," *egnōstai hyp' autou*).[41]

In the concluding lines of the excursus Paul reaffirms the surpassing greatness of love, first, by invoking a formula about "faith, hope, and love" (v. 13). Some such triadic formulation was already part of the apostle's rhetorical repertoire when he wrote 1 Thessalonians (see 1.3; 5.8) – which presumably explains why faith and hope are mentioned along with love, even though neither has come in for special attention in this passage. It is plausible to assume that the Corinthian congregation had heard Paul use this formula, or a variation of it, to summarize what is proper to the new life in Christ. In both of the passages in 1 Thessalonians the terms appear in the sequence, faith – love – hope, which is what one would expect in any comprehensive description of what it means to belong to Christ. In the present context, however, it is understandable that love stands in the third and climactic position,

---

[40] There is doubtless an echo here of Num. 12.6–8, where the knowledge of God granted to prophets in dreams and visions is contrasted with God's speaking with Moses "face to face – clearly, not in riddles" (NRSV). Cf. Exod. 33.11; Deut. 34.10.

[41] In addition to 1 Cor. 8.3, see Gal. 4.9, where Paul again identifies what is decisive for faith, not as coming to know God, but as being known by God (*gnōsthentes hypo theou*).

for love has been the topic of the whole chapter. That Paul identifies love as "the greatest of these" three is consistent with his view of *agapē* as the eschatological reality of God's saving power, by which both faith and hope are called forth and energized; for it is *love*, he says, that "believes all things" and "hopes all things" (v. 7).[42]

Paul's counsels about spiritual gifts bring to a close those sections of 1 Corinthians which contain his most specific appeals and directives. We have seen that certain key theological themes are evident already in the letter's prescript (1.1–3) and opening thanksgiving (1.4–9), and that the apostle both presupposes and enlarges on these in his appeals for congregational unity (in 1.10–4.21), and then as he proceeds to take up various other specific matters pertaining to life in Christ (5.1–11.1 and 11.2–14.40). Arguably, the most definitive theological passages within the body of the letter (through chapter 14) are Paul's excursus on the wisdom of the cross (1.18–2.16); his introduction to the discussion of idol-meats, which includes critically important statements about knowledge and love, as well as the foundational affirmation of "one God . . . and one Lord" (8.1–6); and, in his excursus on the believing community (12.12–13.13), the commendation of love (*agapē*) as "the most excellent way" (12.31–13.13).

Taking these passages together, and in the context of chapters 1–14 as a whole, it becomes evident that the *agapē* Paul commends in chapter 13 is nothing else than the enduring reality of God's own love, which the apostle understands to be revealed in the cross as God's saving power. For the apostle, this love is the reality that is proper to God's own being, and therefore an eschatological power that belongs to an order of reality which is utterly different from the passing realities of this present age. But according to the gospel he had preached in Corinth, and which now informs his letter, in Christ and through the Holy Spirit this eschatological power of God's love has already enlivened the present with God's grace and

---

[42] See also Gal. 5.5–6: hope is nurtured by faith and faith is rendered active by love; Rom. 5.5: hope does not disappoint us, because God's love has been poured out into our hearts through the Holy Spirit. Cf. Söding, *Liebesgebot*, 141.

claimed it for God's purposes. For Paul, it is the saving power and constancy of God's love that engenders faith, nourishes hope, forms and sustains the many into one body, and enables this believing community, as well as each of its members, to experience the reality of "being known by God."

CHAPTER 5

Hoping in God, the "all in all"

If there is any place in 1 Corinthians where doctrinal instruction seems to be Paul's primary aim it is chapter 15, in which his topic is the resurrection of the dead. Two earlier sections of extended theological exposition have supported appeals for a change in conduct; in the case of 1.18–2.16 those appeals are for congregational unity, and in the case of 12.12–13.13 they concern the exercise of spiritual gifts. In chapter 15, however, Paul turns his attention to a matter of *belief*, expressing astonishment that there are "some" in his congregation who do not believe in the resurrection of the dead (v. 12). He does not indicate who or how many were denying this hope, although the extent of his discussion and the evident care with which he has developed his counter arguments suggest that it was probably the majority. It is unclear exactly why the resurrection of the dead was being denied, whether any kind of post-mortem existence was affirmed, and why baptism on behalf of the dead (v. 29) was nonetheless a congregational practice. But uncertainty about these questions does not preclude us from following at least the main lines of the apostle's argument, and thereby enlarging our understanding of the theological orientation of this letter.[1]

However, we must not expect too much. Paul's doctrinal instruction in chapter 15 does not amount to a comprehensive statement of his eschatological views. He is not responding to a request for information about what will happen at the end, or

---

[1] Important, representative studies of this chapter include: Barth, *Resurrection of the Dead*, esp. 107–223; J. Christiaan Beker, *Paul the Apostle: The Triumph of God in Life and Thought* (Philadelphia, 1980), esp. 163–76; Martinus C. De Boer, *The Defeat of Death. Apocalyptic Eschatology in 1 Corinthians 15 and Romans 5*, JSNTSup 22 (Sheffield, 1988); D. B. Martin, *Corinthian Body*, 104–36; Gerhard Sellin, *Der Streit um die Auferstehung der Toten. Eine religionsgeschichtliche und exegetische Untersuchung von 1. Korinther 15*, FRLANT 138 (Göttingen, 1986).

what the consummation of God's purposes will involve, but to a specific doctrinal position that he regards as erroneous. What he says here about the end-time events is incidental to his primary aim, which is to demonstrate that denying the resurrection of the dead contradicts the truth of the gospel on which faith is founded.[2] It is not apparent why he waits until the close of his letter to take up this matter, and he makes no effort to connect it with earlier topics or issues. But what he says here is consistent with the overall eschatological orientation of his gospel, which has been evident from the start, and amounts to an exposition of his earlier statement that "God raised the Lord and will raise us, too, by his power" (6.14). For the apostle, belonging to Christ means belonging as well to the future, and thus living in hope of God's ultimate victory over the death-dealing powers of this present age.

BELONGING TO THE FUTURE

We have seen that by addressing his letter to "God's church" present "in Corinth" (1.2a), Paul has identified his congregation as a community of the end-time which, nevertheless, has a significant present-time vocation. In being formed into a community "sanctified in Christ Jesus" and indwelt by God's Holy Spirit, believers have been called to be "holy people" (1.2bc; 3.16–17), set apart for the service of God. This call and claim of God which they have received in Christ are definitive of their life even while they remain in the world (7.17–24). No less, however, their present belonging to Christ and through him to God (e.g., 1.9; 3.21–23) attest that their ultimate destiny does not lie within this present age, but with the God from whom their life has come ("we exist for him," 8.6). Paul's remarks on both points are infused with a sense of urgency which derives from his conviction that the present age is drawing rapidly to a close (7.29–31; 10.11).[3]

---

[2] This is rightly emphasized by Andreas Lindemann, "Paulus und die korinthische Eschatologie. Zur These von einer 'Entwicklung' im paulinischen Denken," *NTS* 37 (1991), 373–99, here: 386.

[3] A sense of nearness is also suggested by the petition, "Our Lord, come!" (16.22b), which must have originated in Palestinian Christianity (Paul cites it in Aramaic). This was perhaps an element of the church's eucharistic liturgy (cf. 11.26) from a very early date (translated into Greek, it also appears in Rev. 22.20).

Chapters 1–14 also yield evidence of the apostle's more specific eschatological expectations, primarily in the form of statements or references intended to support particular appeals and counsels. Some of these amount to fragments of what he seems to have envisioned as the end-time scenario, while others provide hints of how he conceived the coming salvation itself. Before turning to the related doctrinal instruction in chapter 15, it will be helpful to consider what these earlier remarks suggest about his expectations concerning the end of the present age and the character of the age that is to come.

Four elements of an end-time scenario come into view, although not all at once and with little indication of how Paul may have understood them to be related. (1) As we have already observed, in accord with the expectations of apocalyptic Judaism he anticipates that the closing down of this age will be accompanied by unusual turmoil, disruptions, and distress (7.26–28).[4] (2) The end-time itself will mean "the revealing of our Lord Jesus Christ" (1.7, NRSV; cf. *2 Apoc. Bar.* 39.7), which is to say, his coming again (4.5; 11.26). Paul can therefore describe its inception – borrowing from scriptural announcements of the coming day of Yahweh – as "the day of the Lord" (5.5), or, more elaborately, as "the day of our Lord Jesus Christ" (1.7; cf. 3.13, "the day").[5] (3) At his return the Lord will serve as the agent of God's judgment. On that day he will test the works and disclose the innermost motives of believers, including Paul and others who labor for the gospel (1.8; 3.13; 4.4–5; cf. 11.29–34a), and hold the whole world accountable for its deeds (5.13).[6] Although Paul remarks that "the saints" themselves will participate in the judgment of the world, he does not specify what their particular

---

[4] Above, 65.

[5] Israel's prophets had most often proclaimed "the day of Yahweh" as the day of God's righteous judgment (e.g., Amos 5.18–20; 8.4–10; Isa. 13.6, 9; Joel 1.15; 2.1–2, 11, 31; 3.14; Zeph. 1.7–9, 14–16), but it could also be portrayed as the day of salvation (e.g., Isa. 28.18–19). Later apocalyptic works sometimes identified it specifically as the time of the coming of God's anointed one (e.g., *1 Enoch* 61.5, "the Elect One" will sit in judgment; 2 Esd. 13.52, the "day" of God's "Son").

[6] Unlike prophetic and apocalyptic references to the coming judgment, Paul does not concentrate on the annihilation of those who will be found faithless. He mentions their eschatological destruction only once (3.13–17), without any attendant depiction of its horrors (v. 17; contrast, e.g., Mal. 4.1; *1 Enoch* 102.1–3) and with a remark about being "saved" through fire (v. 15).

function will be (6.2–3). (4) Just as the Lord was raised from the dead, so "God . . . will raise us, too, by his power" (6.14). There is no indication of who precisely the "us" in this statement includes, or of where in the sequence of end-time events the resurrection of the dead is to take place.

Despite his declaration that " 'what God has prepared for those who love him' " has been "revealed to us through the Spirit" (2.9–10, NRSV), in chapters 1–14 Paul offers only a few spare remarks about the hoped-for consummation of God's saving purposes. In one context he describes this as "our glory" (2.7); in another, as gaining an "imperishable wreath" (9.25); and in yet a third he implies that the hope of the faithful is to "inherit God's reign" (6.9–10), which he has earlier identified with the power of God (4.20). The apostle's most deliberate statement about the coming salvation, apart from certain comments in chapter 15, occurs in the context of his commendation of the love that is proper to God's own being, and the one enduring reality (13.12). Here, in keeping with an earlier remark in which knowing God and being saved are essentially parallel conceptions (1.21), he looks forward to knowing God fully and "face to face," even as he has "been known" by God.

It is precarious, on the basis simply of chapters 1–14, to suggest anything more about the eschatological views which inform Paul's thought as we have it in 1 Corinthians. However, even his passing remarks about the end-time and the coming fulfillment of salvation are sufficient to show the thoroughly eschatological orientation of his thought. This is amply confirmed by his extended discussion of the resurrection of the dead which concludes the body of the letter.

THE RESURRECTION OF THE DEAD

Paul's comments in chapter 15 about the resurrection of the dead are fully compatible with the eschatological views he has expressed in chapters 1–14. He has already referred to the resurrection of the dead (6.14); now he seeks to demonstrate why that hope must not be given up. Now, too, he has more to say about the Lord's return (1.7, etc.), which he identifies here as his *parousia* (15.23). Now he writes again about "inheriting" the reign of God (15.50–57; cf. 6.9–10). Earlier he has indicated that humanity's destiny lies with God, from whom all things have come (8.6, "there is one God, the Father, from whom all things exist, and we exist for him"); now he anticipates the eschatological subjection of all things in order that God may be "all in all" (15.28). And here, no less than in the rest of the letter, what he says about the ultimate fulfillment of God's purposes is meant to enhance, not diminish, the significance of the present as a time for the responsible service of God (e.g., 15.58, "So then . . ., be firm, immovable, always excelling in the work of the Lord, knowing that in the Lord your labor is not in vain").

Considering his topic, it is not surprising that the apocalyptic cast of Paul's thought is rather more evident in this chapter than in earlier parts of the letter. His portrayal of "the end," especially what he says about God's final victory over every hostile power (vv. 23–28, 54–55, 57), shows how thoroughly his thinking was steeped in the expectations, terminology, and images of the Jewish apocalyptic tradition. Indeed, he sounds almost like an apocalyptic seer when he says, "Listen carefully, I am telling you a mystery," and then goes on to speak of "the last trumpet" and the wonders it will announce (vv. 51–52). It is therefore all the more striking that in this context Paul says nothing about a final judgment, although it is usually prominent in apocalyptic scenarios and has been mentioned by the apostle himself in earlier parts of the letter. But the omission is a fitting reminder that he has no present interest in providing a comprehensive description of the end-time events.

The apostle's primary aim is to demonstrate both the necessity and the plausibility of believing in the resurrection of the dead. He develops his argument for the necessity of this belief (vv. 12–34) mainly on the basis of the church's tradition, which he cites even before indicating what his topic is (vv. 1–11). He supports his argument that it is also plausible to believe in the resurrection of the dead (vv. 35–49) with analogies from nature as well as an appeal to Scripture. Finally, however, the rhetoric of argument gives way to expressions of wonder and praise (vv. 50–57), and to a pastoral appeal (v. 58). Along the way, several points of special theological interest emerge. In addition to saying that the resurrected Christ is the first fruits of the resurrection of the dead, Paul introduces the notions of a transformed "spiritual body" and of Christ as a second Adam, identifies a role for Christ in facilitating God's reign, and declares that ultimately Christ himself will be subjected to God.

Christ, the first fruits

Paul postpones the actual introduction of his topic, which occurs only in verse 12, in order to issue a solemn reminder about the gospel that he had brought to Corinth and through which his hearers were being saved – if, in fact, they were remaining faithful to it (vv. 1–2). He chooses to summarize this gospel by citing a traditional two-part statement that affirms Christ's death and resurrection (vv. 3b–5). In doing so, however, he significantly extends the list of those to whom the resurrected Christ appeared (vv. 6–8). Somewhat audaciously, he includes himself among these witnesses (v. 8), even though his own encounter with the Lord, when he was called to be an apostle (vv. 9–10; cf. 9.1; Gal. 1.15–17), was perhaps far removed in time from the other appearances he cites.

The listing of so many resurrection appearances may reflect Paul's uncertainty about whether Christ's resurrection was still affirmed in Corinth, or at least about how it was interpreted there. However, when he finally introduces his topic he refers only to the claim that "there is no resurrection of the dead" (v. 12). In responding he seeks to demonstrate, first, that it is absolutely necessary to affirm this doctrine (vv. 13–34). The premise of his argument is evident in v. 20: "The fact is, Christ has been raised from the dead as the first fruits of those who have fallen asleep." Even if Paul does harbor certain doubts about the Corinthians' faith, he seems to assume that by reminding them of the tradition and providing a long list of witnesses he will be able to gain their assent to the proposition that Christ has been raised from the dead. To support the other critical point, that Christ's resurrection is the decisive first installment of a coming resurrection of the dead, he ventures a comparison of Christ and Adam which reflects the view that each is representative of humanity as a whole: "Since death is through a man, also resurrection of the dead is through a man; for as in Adam all die, so also in Christ all will be made alive" (vv. 21–22).

If Paul is serious about this Adam/Christ parallel, and nothing suggests he is not, then he seems to believe that just as all humanity shares in Adam's death, so all who have died – not only those who have embraced the gospel – will share in the resurrection of which Christ is the first fruits. Arguably, had he believed that most of the dead are *not* to be resurrected he would be unable to claim that God will ultimately defeat and destroy even death itself (v. 26; cf. vv. 50–57).[7] But if he expects a resurrection of all the dead, what shall we make of his comment about the sequence of resurrections: "Christ, the first fruits; then at his coming, *those who belong to Christ*" (v. 23)? And what of his assurance in a letter to the Thessalonians, written earlier, that when God's trumpet sounds "the dead *in Christ* will rise first" (1 Thess. 4.16, NRSV)? As for the latter, Paul's usage elsewhere suggests (contra NRSV) that "in Christ" should be read with the verb it precedes, not with the noun it follows. If so, then the apostle would not be saying that only *the dead in Christ* will rise, but that the dead *will rise in Christ* (cf. "through Jesus," 1 Thess. 4.14b).[8]

As for the comment here in chapter 15 (v. 23), nothing requires us to suppose that Paul's reference to "those who belong to Christ" reflects his belief that *only* those will be resurrected. In fact, the context suggests otherwise. Verse 23 reformulates verse 20, where, in his first statement about Christ as the first fruits, Paul refers without any qualification to the resurrection of "those who have fallen asleep." Moreover, it directly follows his emphatic declaration that "all" will be made alive in Christ (v. 22b). After this twofold statement (vv. 20, 21–22) of his fundamental point that Christ's resurrection guarantees the resurrection of ("all") the dead, Paul registers it yet again (v. 23), but now with specific reference to "those who belong to Christ." It is not likely that he means to qualify what he has just said so emphatically and without qualification. More likely, he is picking up from where he had been in verses 17–19, focused on the situation in Corinth. If the members of his congregation "have hoped in Christ about this life only," they are more pitiable than unbelievers, who live without hoping in Christ even

[7] So also, e.g., Barth, *Resurrection of the Dead*, 175; De Boer, *The Defeat of Death*, 112; Lindemann, "Paulus und die korinthische Eschatologie," 383–84.
[8] Thus Lindemann, "Paulus und die korinthische Eschatologie," 379.

for this life (v. 19). But they need not be more pitiable than unbelievers, for as believers their hope can be founded on the certainty
that Christ has been raised from the dead as the first fruits of their
own resurrection.

To be sure, most interpreters maintain, or else simply presume,
that Paul expects the resurrection only of the Christian dead, and
this possibility cannot be ruled out.[9] The evidence is not clear-cut,
one way or the other, precisely because the destiny of the non-
Christian dead is not one of the points at issue. Indeed, whether the
apostle expects the resurrection of "all" without qualification or
only of "all who have believed in Christ," his premise that Christ is
the first fruits still supports the argument he is working out: (1) When
the Corinthians claim "there is no resurrection of the dead" they are
also denying that Christ has been raised (vv. 13, 15–16). (2) In denying
that Christ has been raised they are thereby contradicting the gospel
Paul has proclaimed to them (v. 14; cf. vv. 1–11). (3) In contradicting
Paul's gospel they are simultaneously contradicting their own faith,
which was generated by that gospel (v. 14), and also their professed
knowledge of the God to whom Paul has borne witness (v. 15; cf. v.
34; 8.1–6; 12.2). (4) If their faith is invalid they are "still in their sins,"
and even their present life is all futility (vv. 17–19; cf. vv. 30–34).

In the course of developing these points Paul digresses to remark
on what else will happen when Christ returns and the dead are
raised (vv. 24–28). Although this brief aside does not contribute
directly to Paul's argument, it is important for what it discloses
about his view of God's final victory. However, this is a topic we
may best consider when Paul himself returns to it at the close of
his discussion (vv. 50–57).

The spiritual body, a second Adam

Paul seems to know that his argument for the necessity of believing in the resurrection of the dead will not be persuasive unless he

---

[9] E.g., Barrett, *First Epistle*, 352, 355; Conzelmann, *1 Corinthians*, 268 n. 49; 269, 270; Fee,
First Epistle, 751; Richard B. Hays, *First Corinthians*, Interpretation (Louisville, KY, 1997),
264; Sellin, *Der Streit*, 270. C. E. Hill agrees that the topic in chapter 15 is the resurrection
of believers, yet allows that Paul may also have expected others to be raised up, only not
to redemption and life ("Paul's Understanding of Christ's Kingdom in 1 Corinthians
15:20–28," *NovT* 30 [1988], 297–320, here: 304–307).

can also demonstrate that it is plausible. In particular, to his primarily Gentile congregation he must demonstrate that the dead can be raised to life even though the "natural body" (*sōma psychikon*) with which one is born will decay and disappear. He appeals initially to what can be observed in nature, then subsequently to what Scripture attests. Underlying the first is his understanding of God as beneficent Creator, and underlying the second is his understanding of Christ as the agent of God's saving power.

The appeal to consider what happens in nature (vv. 36–41) is more accurately described as an appeal to consider what God has provided for in the created order. In this connection, Paul's most critical point is that God has chosen to give each form of existence its own distinctive body (*sōma*, v. 38). Indeed, each of the forms he mentions (vv. 37, 39–41) is named as well in the creation account of Genesis 1 (plants yielding seeds, Gen. 1.11–12; human beings, Gen. 1.26–27; animals, birds, and fish, Gen. 1.20–25; the sun, moon, and stars, Gen. 1.14–18). Paul's comments here, like his earlier statements about God's providential arrangement of the parts of the body (12.18, 24b), reflect an understanding of God as both the Creator of all that is and as being concerned that all things flourish. This also holds for what the apostle asks his audience to observe about the "bare seed" that "dies" when planted, but is subsequently "made alive" (vv. 36–37).

Applying this to the case at hand, Paul draws an analogy between the seed that dies, only to be made alive, and the resurrection of the dead (vv. 42–44). Although the "natural body" perishes, it will be replaced, he says, by a new "spiritual body" (*sōma pneumatikon*, v. 44a). Just as there is first a seed that dies and then a flourishing plant, so there is first a natural body and then a spiritual one (v. 44b). This notion contrasts sharply with the widespread Hellenistic belief, perhaps no less the prevailing view among the members of Paul's congregation, that if there is any life beyond death it can only be some type of spiritualized, disembodied existence. For the apostle, however, there can be no true existence apart from the "body" (*sōma*), by which he means the *whole person* (including, but not only, the perishable "flesh and blood," v. 50), whose identity is given and consists in the enduring reality of being known by God and belonging to Christ. Therefore, when he refers to the resurrection of the body (*sōma*) he is affirming that one continues, in all of one's individuality, to be "known" by God. And when he describes the resurrection body as spiritual (*pneumatikon*) he is affirming that it has been raised "imperishable" and "in glory" (vv. 42, 43), to another order of existence.

In further support of his claim that when the dead are resurrected the "spiritual" (*pneumatikos*) will replace the "natural" (*psychikos*), Paul again compares Adam and Christ (vv. 45–49), but now on the basis of a specific scriptural text. In part, it would seem that he wants to correct an interpretation of Genesis 2.7 which held that Adam was created as not only "the first" but also the ideal human being, although he lost that status when he disobeyed God. This view is found in the writings of Philo and elsewhere, and may well have been held in Corinth, too.[10] Paul insists, to the contrary, that not Adam but Christ, the "second man" and "last Adam," is the one in whom humanity is to find its destiny. Whereas God created Adam from the dust, Christ has come from heaven; thus the "natural" was first and the "spiritual" is second.[11]

Paul's statement of the matter accentuates another and equally decisive way the second man is different from the first. Whereas Adam *received* life and became a "living being" (*psychēn zōsan*, quoting Gen. 2.7), Christ *bestows* life because he is a "life-giving spirit" (*pneuma zōopoioun*). This description of Christ tells us nothing about the apostle's reflections, if he had any, concerning the relation of Christ to the Spirit. However, it most certainly reflects his understanding of Christ himself as the agent of God's saving power. From a scriptural point of view only God can "make alive" (*zōopoiein*; in the Greek Bible, see, especially, Neh. 9.6; Ps. 71.20), as the apostle himself is quite aware (6.14; 15.15; cf. 2 Cor. 4.13–14).[12] Correspondingly, both times Adam is mentioned here (vv. 21–22,

---

[10] In addition to the commentaries, see, e.g., De Boer, *The Defeat of Death*, 96–105, 128–32; Romano Penna, "Adamic Christology and Anthropological Optimism in 1 Corinthians 15:45–49," *Paul the Apostle*, I.206–31, here: 211–26.

[11] C. K. Barrett suggests that when Paul describes Christ as "the man from heaven" he is thinking of Dan. 7.13, which envisions the coming from heaven of "one like a son of man" (NRSVmg.); see "The Significance of the Adam-Christ Typology for the Resurrection of the Dead: 1 Cor 15: 20–22, 45–49," repr. in *Jesus and the Word and Other Essays*, Princeton Theological Monograph Series 4 (Allison Park, PA, 1995), 163–84, here: 177–79. But even if Barrett is right, our understanding of Pauline christology is not significantly advanced.   [12] Cf. Penna, "Adamic Christology," 218–22.

45–49) he is viewed as the agent of death. Writing to the Romans several years later, Paul will specify that death is the consequence of sin, which through Adam's trespass came to exercise its dominion over the whole of humanity (5.12–21). In the present context, however, the topic is not sin but Christ as the first fruits of the resurrection of the dead. It is only in order to explain this connection that Paul compares Christ with Adam, and for this purpose it is enough to present Adam as the representative human whose death is shared by the whole of humankind.

In concluding this comparison of Adam and Christ (vv. 48–49), Paul shifts his focus to the humankind of which they are the representative figures. Because every human being has been created mortal, he can declare that humanity presently bears "the image of the man of dust" (cf. Gen. 1.27). But he is equally emphatic that those who now bear the image of Adam *shall* bear the image of Christ, "the man of heaven."[13] The latter remains a hope, but one made certain because Christ, as "life-giving spirit" and the first fruits of the resurrection of the dead, imprints the present with the "already" of God's saving power.[14]

GOD'S FINAL VICTORY

Summing up his comments about the spiritual body with which the dead will be raised, Paul declares that only the imperishable can inherit the coming reign of God (v. 50). But this statement, like his entire discussion of the resurrection of the dead, forces a question that he has not addressed so far. What about those who will not die before Christ returns (among whom he seems to include himself, v. 51), and who will therefore still be bearing "the image of the man of dust"? His answer constitutes an addendum to the argument, and moves it quickly toward its conclusion.

Paul's comment about those who will survive until the end is in the form of an apocalyptic pronouncement, a disclosure of the "mystery" that when the last trumpet sounds "all of us will be

---

[13] With Barrett, *First Epistle*, 377–78, and others, I take the context to support the future tense (*phoresomen*) over the hortatory subjunctive (*phoresōmen*, adopted, e.g., by Fee, *First Epistle*, 794–95), although the latter is admittedly better attested.

[14] Penna, "Adamic Christology," 230.

changed" (v. 51). He means that just as the dead will be raised with imperishable, spiritual bodies, so too the living will be clothed with immortality (vv. 52–53). The image of *putting on* imperishability (immortality) like new clothing (vv. 53, 54) derives from the Jewish apocalyptic tradition (note, e.g., *1 Enoch* 62.15; 1QS iv.7–8), and reflects a conception of life after death that is sharply at odds with the popular Hellenistic view, which held that immortality requires putting *off* the material and corruptible garment of flesh. It is significant that Paul says nothing about putting off the flesh (*sarx*), much less the body (*sōma*). Indeed, his comments about the mystery of "change" and putting *on* a new form of existence presume a fundamental continuity of identity (*sōma*) for the subject who is thus transformed.

In order to emphasize that with this transformation death will be utterly and forever destroyed, Paul cites the promise in Isaiah 25.7 that death will be "swallowed up in victory," and the mocking questions in Hosea 13.14, "O Death, where is your victory? O Death, where is your sting?" (vv. 54–55). It is impossible to determine whether the apostle himself is responsible for conflating these texts and giving them the form they have here.[15] However this may be, as he cites them they portray death as an adversary who is destined to be completely overwhelmed by God's invincible power.

Along with the reference to God's coming reign (v. 50), the affirmation of God's ultimate victory over death returns us to the apocalyptic scenario suggested by Paul's remarks in vv. 24–28, where he has said that death will be "the last enemy" destroyed (v. 26).[16] He probably has in mind that mysterious instant when, simultaneously, the dead will be resurrected imperishable and the living will be clothed with immortality (vv. 51–53). Calling on Psalms 110.1 and 8.6 (vv. 24–25, 27, 28a), he envisions that final

---

[15] For discussions see, e.g., Fee, *First Epistle*, 803–805; Traugott Holtz, "νῖκος," *EDNT*, II.468–69.

[16] Special studies include: Uta Heil, "Theo-logische Interpretation von 1 Kor 15, 23–28," *ZNW* 84 (1993), 27–35; Hill, "Christ's Kingdom"; Jan Lambrecht, "Structure and Line of Thought in 1 Cor. 15, 23–28," repr. in *Pauline Studies: Collected Essays*, BETL 115 (Leuven, 1994), 161–73; Andreas Lindemann, "Parusie Christi und Herrschaft Gottes: Zur Exegese von 1 Kor 15, 23–28," *WD*, n. F. 19 (1987), 87–107; Thüsing, *Gott und Christus*, 238–54.

victory as the culmination of God's campaign to bring "every rule and authority and power" under subjection to Christ (cf. 2.6).[17]

As the apostle presents it, Christ's role in this cosmic unfolding of God's saving purposes is to serve as God's vice-regent, reigning until God has put every tyrannical force in subjection to him. This is a variation of the traditional apocalyptic expectation that a temporary kingdom ruled by the Messiah will precede the coming of God's kingdom in its fullness (e.g., 2 Esd. 7.26–31; 23.31–34; *2 Apoc. Bar.* 29.1–30.5; Rev. 19.11–21.8). According to Paul, the reign of Christ is already present (see, esp., v. 25), having been inaugurated with Christ's resurrection, and is destined to continue until he returns.[18] Described apocalyptically, as here, this is the period when the power of God, exercised through the vice-regency of the resurrected-crucified Christ, is in the process of challenging and defeating the rulers of the present, passing age.[19] Paul therefore views the present as standing already under the promise of "the end," when God's victory will be complete. Even now, despite the struggles, threats, and sufferings that accompany life in this world, believers are liberated and claimed by the inbreaking power of the reign of God.

And indeed, Paul is writing about *God's* reign, not about the reign of Christ.[20] Although it is Christ who presently reigns (*basileuein*, v. 25), the reign as such (*[hē] basileia*, vv. 24, 50) belongs to

---

[17] Because of the apostle's dependence on Pss. 110.1 and 8.6, which had likely been combined already in the pre-Pauline tradition (see, esp., Eph. 1.20–22; 1 Pet. 3.22), the subjects of some of the verbs are difficult to determine. In my judgment, God (not Christ) is the intended subject in all of the disputed cases (vv. 24b, 25, and 27a, where NRSV has, respectively, "he has destroyed," "he has put," "God has put"). This accords not only with the viewpoint of the Psalms that are quoted, but also with Paul's own viewpoint as expressed in v. 28b (where "the one who put all things in subjection" [NRSV] has to be God) and the chapter as a whole (where he emphasizes that God is the one who raises the dead and achieves the final victory). The arguments for this conclusion are given most fully by Heil, "Theo-logische Interpretation." For arguments against it, see Lambrecht, "1 Cor. 15, 23–28."

[18] Hill, "Christ's Kingdom," esp. 310–20, shows why chiliastic interpretations, which view Christ's reign as commencing only with his *parousia*, must be ruled out.

[19] Cf. Wolfgang Schrage, "Der gekreuzigte und auferweckte Herr. Zur theologia crucis und theologia resurrectionis bei Paulus," *ZTK* 94 (1997), 25–38, here: 35–37.

[20] The phrase, "reign of Christ," appears neither in 1 Corinthians nor in any of the other letters of undisputed Pauline authorship. See, however, Eph. 5.5 (the unrighteous will not inherit "the reign of Christ and of God") and Col. 1.13 (God has transferred believers "into the reign of his beloved Son").

God. The theocentric orientation of Paul's thought, here as well as
throughout the letter, is especially evident in the statements that
frame verses 24–28. At the end Christ will deliver the reign to "God
the Father" (v. 24a), and then Christ himself – "the Son" (cf. 1.9) –
will be subjected to the Father, "that God may be all in all" (v.
28bc). This theme of Christ's own subjection has surfaced twice
before in other forms, somewhat incidentally in 11.3 ("and God is
the head of Christ"), and with special emphasis in 3.22b–23:
"everything belongs to you, and you belong to Christ, and Christ
belongs to God." It would be anachronistic, however, to conclude
from these passages that Paul had worked out a "subordinationist"
christology. In each case, and especially here in chapter 15, his
attention is focused less on the status of Christ and his relation to
God than on the truth about God himself, to which he makes
specific reference in v. 15.[21] The apostle's vision is of God as ultimately "all in all," by which he does not mean that "all things" (*ta
panta*, v. 28b) will be somehow taken up *into* God, but that God will
be established in unrivaled sovereignty *over* all things.[22] Subjection
to God therefore involves a particular *relationship* with him, which
is why Paul must insist that only an embodied existence suffices for
participating in God's reign.

Paul's statement about the ultimate subjection of all things to
God must be interpreted in accord with the understanding of God
that we have encountered throughout this letter. He most certainly
does not think of God as a tyrant who establishes himself in power
by exploiting and controlling others. In that case, how could he
speak of God's final victory as a hope? To the contrary, in proclaiming that the cross is the place of God's definitive self-disclosure he has identified the power that is proper to God's own being
as the saving power of love, which is present as both a gift and a
claim in Christ's giving himself for others. It is therefore not unreasonable to conclude that when Paul envisions the subjection of all

---

[21] Also noted by Ulrich Luz, *Das Geschichtsverständnis des Paulus*, BEvT 49 (München, 1968),
351–52.
[22] In Paul's day, descriptions of God as "the all" or "all in all" were most common in circles
where pantheistic or mystical views were espoused. But such formulas are also found in
the literature of Hellenistic Judaism, where, as in 1 Cor. 15.28, they were used to express
the awesome sovereignty of the Creator over creation (e.g., Sir. 43.27–33). See
Conzelmann, *1 Corinthians*, 275.

things to God he is thinking of their subjection without let or hindrance to God's love – presumably, within that same new order of existence where one will know God fully, just as one has already "been fully known" by God's electing love (13.12).

As the apostle draws his discussion to a close, his confidence that God's love will prevail wells up into an expression of thanks "to God who gives us the victory through our Lord Jesus Christ" (v. 57). It is clear that the "victory" Paul refers to is God's ultimate defeat of death, as attested by the prophetic oracles he has just cited (vv. 54b–55). It is less clear why he pauses, after introducing the scriptural texts, to explain that sin is death's "sting" and that the law is sin's power (v. 56).[23] However consistent this remark may be with what he says in Romans about the law, sin, and death (e.g., 5.12–13; 7.9–13), it seems rather out of place in 1 Corinthians, where the law is scarcely mentioned and where there is no conception of sin as a power except in this one, isolated sentence.[24] Still, there is no reason to attribute the comment to a later hand, as some interpreters have, because it is well enough explained as Paul's exegetic gloss on the word "sting" in Hosea 13.14. Perhaps with Adam again in mind, he takes the opportunity to identify sin as the means through which humanity is infected with mortality (Gen. 2.17) – adding, as if to round off the thought, that sin is empowered by the law. This is important evidence that Paul has already been pondering the role of the law and its relation to sin and death, although his statement is so compact that it is hard to judge whether his thinking on the matter is already as developed as it appears to be by the time of Romans.

Read simply as a comment on the text from Hosea, the apostle's linking of death and sin and his mention of sin's empowerment call

---

[23] In addition to the commentaries, see, e.g., H. W. Hollander and J. Holleman, "Death, Sin, and Law in 1 Cor 15:56," *NovT* 35 (1993), 270–91; Thomas Söding, "'Die Kraft der Sünde ist das Gesetz' (1Kor 15,56). Anmerkungen zum Hintergrund und zur Pointe einer gesetzeskritischen Sentenz des Apostels Paulus," *ZNW* 83 (1992), 74–84; Frank Thielman, "The Coherence of Paul's View of the Law: The Evidence of First Corinthians," *NTS* 38 (1992), 235–53.

[24] Apart from references to "the law" of Scripture (9.8, 9; 14.21, 34), the law is mentioned only in 9.20–21, where Paul remarks that even though he is not "under the law" he is also not "without the law as respects God," because he is "in-lawed to Christ" (9.20–21). The other references to sin(s), etc. in 1 Corinthians are all incidental to Paul's discussion of other topics (6.18; 7.28, 36; 8.12; 15.3, 17, 34).

attention to the existential reality of death's present grip even on the living. Correspondingly, it is the significance of God's final victory for humanity, as its liberation from sin and death, that is expressed in his offering of thanks to God – "who *gives us* the victory." This victory belongs to God, but it is not for God alone. Because it is the victory of God's sovereign, saving love, it is also for "us" and the whole of creation. Paul's use of the present tense reflects his belief that God's final victory is certain, but even more particularly that its certainty is assured by what God has already accomplished "through our Lord Jesus Christ." Given the course of his argument, he could be thinking specifically of Christ as the "first fruits" of the resurrection of the dead and the "last Adam" who became a "life-giving spirit." Yet for Paul, the one whom God has raised from the dead and through whom God's victory is won remains the *crucified* Christ, and the cross remains the place where God's will and power to save are definitively revealed (1.18–2.16). A crown has not replaced the cross as emblematic of God's power, nor has Christ's resurrection canceled out his crucifixion. Rather, in raising Christ from the dead God has *confirmed* and *established* the cross as the definitive and continuing norm for life in Christ.[25]

Having completed his argument and expressed his thanks to God, Paul concludes with an appeal to the congregation (v. 58), urging it to excel "in the Lord's work [*en tō ergō tou kyriou*], knowing that in the Lord" its labor is not in vain. Elsewhere he refers to the congregation itself as the Lord's work (*ergon*), founded and built up through the labors of his ministers (3.5–15; 9.1; 16.10).[26] The present call to "excel" (*perisseuein*) in this work is therefore function-ally equivalent to his earlier appeal to "try to excel [*perisseuein*] in building up the church" (14.12), which is precisely his own objec-tive in this letter.

If the Corinthians have been attentive to what the apostle has been saying, they will hear in his appeal to excel in the Lord's work another call to become agents of the love with which God has graced and claimed them in Christ, for he has emphasized more

---

[25] Cf. De Boer, *The Defeat of Death*, 140; Wolfgang Schrage, "1. Korinther 15, 1–11," *Résurrection du Christ et des chrétiens (1 Co 15)*, Benedictina, Biblical-ecumenical section, 8 (ed. by Lorenzo de Lorenzi; Rome, 1985), 21–45, here: 27, 30.

[26] Wolff, *Der erste Brief*, 420; cf. Barrett, *First Epistle*, 385.

than once that love is what "builds up." In case they have been less than attentive, he issues this call quite directly when drawing the letter to a close: "Let everything you do be done in love" (16.14; cf. 14.26c). One can imagine contexts in which this very general appeal would amount to little more than an encouragement to be kind to others. But here it is invested with the full weight of Paul's gospel as that comes to expression in 1 Corinthians. The love he has in view is the *agapē* that is proper to God's own being, which both graces and claims the whole of creation and has been revealed in the saving power of the cross. In their belonging to the resurrected-crucified Christ, believers are formed into a community that lives from the cross and are called to be agents of God's love, both individually and corporately, within the particularities of their own time and place. Despite the complexities, ambiguities, threats, and terrors that may confront them, they can know "that in the Lord [their] labor is not in vain," because in the end the victory belongs to God, who is sovereign in love and "all in all."

CHAPTER 6

The significance of 1 Corinthians for Christian thought

It is customary to describe 1 and 2 Corinthians, Galatians, and Romans as the four "main" Pauline letters. In part, this description reflects the fact that they are longer than the other three letters generally accepted as authentic, but primarily it reflects the widespread judgment that Paul's theology is most fully and carefully presented in Galatians and Romans, while his apostolic self-understanding and views on practical, moral issues are most readily discerned in 1 and 2 Corinthians. However, these common judgments need to be modified in several respects.

First, no one or two Pauline letters can be absolutely definitive either of the apostle's thought or of his ministry. Each letter provides no more than a snapshot of what he was thinking and doing within one particular period of time and one specific set of circumstances.

Second, the other three letters of unquestionably Pauline authorship – 1 Thessalonians, Philippians, and Philemon – are surely no less important for being shorter. All three contribute substantially to our understanding of Paul's message and mission.

Third, it is precisely by considering all of the letters together, within their various situational contexts, that one is able to get some measure of how the individual snapshots can contribute to a larger panoramic view of the apostle's understanding and preaching of the gospel. Whether it is possible to document any significant change or development in his theology and pastoral strategies remains a matter of spirited debate among interpreters; but one must allow at least for the possibility that over time there was some change in these.

Finally, the present study of theology in 1 Corinthians has shown how wrong it would be to regard this particular letter as significant mainly for what it discloses about Paul's pastoral work and teachings, and only marginally important for what it discloses about his theological point of view. Arguably, 1 Corinthians is an even better place to take the apostle's theological pulse than the allegedly "more theological" letters to the Galatians and Romans, because here it is especially evident not only that his thinking about the gospel took shape within the crucible of his missionary and pastoral labors, but also how it did so. Paul's theological legacy is not a systematic theology, or even a collection of doctrinal building blocks from which a theological system might be constructed. That legacy is complex, of course, but we come close to the heart of it in his clear-sighted identification of the gospel with the saving power of God's love as disclosed in Christ, and his insistence that those who are called to belong to Christ are thereby summoned to be agents of God's love wherever in the world they have received that call. Herein lies the integrity of "theology" and "ethics" in Paul's thought, and this is what one sees with special clarity in 1 Corinthians.

To be sure, 1 Corinthians has also contributed to Christian thought in more specific ways. Some of these can be indicated by briefly considering how this letter is distinctive within the New Testament, and how it has been important for the church across the centuries.

1 CORINTHIANS IN THE NEW TESTAMENT

Of the thirteen writings which comprise the so-called "Pauline corpus" within the New Testament, only 1 Thessalonians is certainly earlier than 1 Corinthians, although Galatians may well be, too. The remaining letters, including all those of disputed authorship, are certainly later. Any judgment about how far Paul's theological outlook in 1 Corinthians may assume, specifically continue, or differ from views he expressed in earlier letters, and how far it may still be evident in his later letters, would necessarily involve us in issues that are too complex to be explored here. It is a much easier task, however, and no less important, to observe what is most theologically distinctive about 1 Corinthians when it is compared, especially, with the other letters generally agreed to be from the apostle himself. In considering this, we may be guided by the four traditional doctrinal topics that were invoked at the beginning of this study in order to summarize the areas in which the views of the Corinthians were in tension with Paul's own: christology, soteriology, eschatology, and ecclesiology.

Christology

We have seen that there is no more compelling christological image in 1 Corinthians than the one Paul introduces near the beginning of the letter when he identifies God's saving power with the cross and emphasizes that he has preached only "Jesus Christ, and him crucified." The image of Christ crucified is equally prominent in Galatians (see, esp., Gal. 3.1), but in that (earlier?) letter the apostle does not accord it such deliberate and sustained attention as he does in 1 Corinthians 1.18–2.16. Moreover and more particularly, although Galatians is no less important than 1 Corinthians as a source for what interpreters have long described as Paul's *theologia crucis* (theology of the cross), the letter to Corinth is distinctive in reflecting, as well, what has been called his *theologia resurrectionis* (theology of the resurrection). Our letter thus forces the question, in a way that Galatians does not, of how these two important Pauline themes are related.[1] What 1 Corinthians shows, as no other letter does so effectively, is that Paul perceives God's saving power to be disclosed both in Jesus' death (1.18, 21–25) and in his resurrection from the dead (6.14; 15.15), and that it is the crucified Christ whom God has resurrected as Lord, to reign until all of God's enemies have been destroyed.

Apart from Galatians and 1 Corinthians, Paul uses the language of "cross" and "crucifixion" only in Philippians 2.8b (a Pauline gloss on a hymnic reference to Jesus' death specifies that it was on a cross), 3.18 (purveyors of false teaching are "enemies of the cross of Christ," NRSV), and Romans 6.6 (the "old self" [NRSV] is crucified with Christ). There are but three references to the cross

---

[1] This is the special topic of Schrage's essay, "Der gekreuzigte und auferweckte Herr." For his comments on 1 Corinthians, see, esp., 29–38.

in the disputed letters, where it is associated, respectively, with reconciliation (Col. 1.20, of all things; Eph. 2.16, of Jews and Gentiles) and the forgiveness of trespasses (Col. 2.14). Elsewhere in the New Testament, apart from the passion narratives in the Gospels, there are scattered references to Jesus' crucifixion (Matt. 20.19; Luke 24.7, 20; Acts 2.36; 4.10; Heb. 6.6; 12.2; Rev. 11.8; cf. Matt. 23.34), and references to the cross in several sayings about discipleship (Mark 8.34/Matt. 16.24/Luke 9.23; Matt. 10.38; Luke 14.27). Yet nowhere in the New Testament is the image of the resurrected-crucified Christ so finely drawn and so important for the argument as in 1 Corinthians.

Two other noteworthy images emerge in Paul's discussion of the resurrection of the dead, where he portrays Christ as both the "first fruits" and a second Adam. By describing Christ as the "first fruits" (*aparchē*) of those who have died (15.20, 23) he means to emphasize that Christ's own resurrection inaugurates the resurrection of the dead, which may therefore be embraced as a hope certainly to be fulfilled (cf. 6.14; 15.15). As applied to Christ, this image is unique to 1 Corinthians, although Paul's comment in Romans about believers having "the first fruits of the Spirit" (8.23) as a sure hope of the "redemption" of their bodies (cf. 1 Cor. 15) is closely related. The kind of link between Christ's resurrection and the resurrection of the dead that is forged by this image is perhaps anticipated in 1 Thessalonians 4.14 (cf. 5.10), and is likely presupposed in 2 Corinthians 4.14 (cf. 13.4) and Romans 8.11 (cf. 14.9).

Paul's identification of Christ as a second Adam (15.21–22, 45–47) is closely related to his portrayal of him as the first fruits of the resurrection of the dead. While the first Adam brought death, "the last Adam" brings life; while the first Adam, who was created from the dust, became a living being, "the second man," who is from heaven, became a life-giving spirit. Some such comparison may be reflected in the hymn of Philippians 2.6–11,[2] but the only other place it is explicit in the Pauline corpus is Romans 5.12–21. In Romans, too, Paul identifies Adam with death (vv. 12, 14, 15, 17, 21) and Christ with life (vv. 17, 18, 21), although in Romans the comparison is not

---

[2] E.g., Morna D. Hooker, "Philippians 2.6–11," repr. in *From Adam to Christ. Essays on Paul* (Cambridge, 1990), 88–100; Peter T. O'Brien, *The Epistle to the Philippians: A Commentary on the Greek Text*, NIGTC (Grand Rapids, 1991), 263–68.

developed by referring to Christ as "the last Adam," "the second man," or "the man from heaven," but by references to "the one [man], Jesus Christ" (vv. 15, 17) and "[the] one man" (vv. 18, 19). More significantly, in Romans Paul goes beyond what he has said in 1 Corinthians by associating death with Adam's sin (e.g., vv. 12, 14–16) and sin with the law (vv. 13, 20), and by speaking of Christ's "obedience" which brings "rectification" and "righteousness" (5.15–17, 18–19, 21). There is no similar exposition of the law, sin, and death anywhere in 1 Corinthians, no reference to Christ's death as an act of obedience, and only summary mentions of righteousness (1.30) and rectification (6.11; cf. 4.4; 15.34). Interpreters differ on whether Paul's comment that sin is death's sting and the law is sin's power (1 Cor. 15.56) only anticipates the views he will spell out in Romans 5 or is evidence that his views on the law, sin, and death were already essentially formed by the time he wrote 1 Corinthians. Of course, the latter is almost certainly the case if Galatians antedates 1 Corinthians, because the views expressed in Romans are clearly anticipated in Galatians.

Although Adam is also referred to in Jude 14 (as the progenitor of humankind) and 1 Timothy 2.13–14 (where Eve, not Adam, is named as the transgressor), neither passage is christologically significant. However, the one remaining New Testament reference to Adam occurs in Luke's genealogy of Jesus, where Jesus' lineage is traced, finally, to "Enos, son of Seth, son of Adam, son of God" (Luke 3.38, NRSV). This identification of Adam as "son of God" may presuppose a comparison with Jesus, who is addressed several times in Luke as "the son of God" (3.22; 4.3, 9), but even if it does the genealogy itself affords little help in determining what the comparison was meant to show.[3]

Finally, the christological orientation of 1 Corinthians is distinguished by the way in which Paul speaks of Christ's relation to God. We have noted three explicit statements of this, which occur in three separate contexts. Near the beginning of the letter, stressing that believers belong to Christ, he extends his point by adding

[3] See R. Alan Culpepper, "The Gospel of Luke," *NIB* 9 (ed. by L. E. Keck *et al.*; Nashville, 1995), 1–490, here: 95; Robert C. Tannehill, *Luke*, ANTC (Nashville, 1996), 86–87; C. F. Evans, *Saint Luke*, TPI New Testament Commentaries (London and Philadelphia, 1990), 253.

that "Christ belongs to God" (*Christos de theou*, 3.23: a genitive of belonging). Later, remarking that the head of a woman is a man, he adds that "God is the head of Christ" (11.3, NRSV). And near the close of the letter he declares that when Christ "hands over the reign" to his Father, "the Son himself will be subjected [to him], that God may be all in all" (15.24, 28). Not only are there no comparably pointed expressions in the other letters of undisputed Pauline authorship, but in Philippians 3.21 the apostle apparently regards Christ himself as the one who subjects all things. Moreover, in the disputed letters there is a marked tendency to attribute to Christ what the undisputed letters attribute to God. In Colossians, for example, Christ is declared to be invested with the fullness of God (1.19; 2.9), and in both Colossians and Ephesians Christ himself is acclaimed as the "head over all things" (Eph. 1.20–22, NRSV; cf. Col. 1.18–19; 2.10) and the "all in all" (Col. 3.11; Eph. 1.23).

Soteriology

We have noted previously that Paul never employs the noun "salvation" in 1 Corinthians, only verbal forms, and that he is at some pains to disabuse his Corinthian congregation of the notion that the fullness of salvation can be experienced in this present age, even though he affirms that God's saving power is already present and at work through Christ. In these respects 1 Corinthians is not much different from the other unquestionably Pauline letters. It is also the case that here as elsewhere the apostle has made use of several traditional terms and formulas to express the means and character of salvation; notably, "Christ died for our sins" (15.3; cf. 5.7b; 8.11), and Christ is our "righteousness," "sanctification," and "redemption" (1.30; cf. 6.11). But despite a certain emphasis on God's sanctifying action in Christ and the community's being called to holiness, 1 Corinthians is more notable for what is not said about these traditional themes than for any distinctive treatment of them.

To the extent that 1 Corinthians presents a distinctive understanding of salvation, this is especially evident in Paul's exposition of the cross as disclosing the power and wisdom of God. In that context, "being saved" means being delivered from the folly that attends humanity's ultimately futile and self-destructive attempt to know God through its own finite wisdom. Expressed more positively, it means being freed to belong to Christ and through him to God, whom one will come to know fully – when all things are wholly subjected to God's saving love – as one has already "been known" by God. Although the idea of being called to belong to Christ is by no means unique to 1 Corinthians, the idea is especially prominent and often strikingly expressed in this letter, as we have seen (e.g., 1.9; 3.23; and the imagery of being bought with a price/being a slave of Christ, 6.19b–20; 7.22–23). Moreover, while knowing (and being known by) God is an important theme throughout Paul's letters (e.g., 1 Thess. 1.10; 4.5; Gal. 4.8–9; 2 Cor. 4.6; Rom. 1.19–25; cf. 8.29–30), it is only in 1 Corinthians that knowing/being known by God is explicitly linked with the relationship initiated, defined, and fulfilled by the saving power of God's love (8.1–3; 13.8–12). There is also no similar linking of knowledge and love elsewhere in the New Testament, except perhaps in the literature of the Johannine tradition (e.g., John 17.25–26; 1 John 2.3–6; 4.7–12; cf. John 10.1–18).[4]

Eschatology

The eschatological outlook in 1 Corinthians is distinguished primarily by what Paul has to say in chapter 15 about the end-time events, especially Christ's turning over the reign to God, the bestowal of a "spiritual body," and what will happen to those who are still alive when Christ returns.

Although the conception of a "reign" of Christ is expressed or implied elsewhere in the New Testament besides 1 Corinthians (e.g., Matt. 25.31–46; John 18.33–37; Col. 1.13; Eph. 5.5; 2 Tim. 4.1, 18; 2 Pet. 1.11; Rev. 1.5; 11.15; 19.11–21.8; cf. Luke 23.42), the idea that Christ will ultimately turn over the reign to God and then himself be subjected to God appears only here (15.24–28). As we have seen, Paul refers to Christ's reigning as a present

---

[4] Cf. Bertil E. Gärtner, "The Pauline and Johannine Idea of 'To Know God' Against the Hellenistic Background," *NTS* 14 (1968), 209–31.

reality, having begun with his resurrection and destined to continue until his *parousia* and the defeat of death. This is a very different understanding from the one reflected in Revelation 19.11–21.8, where the seer envisions a thousand-year reign of Christ that will begin, not conclude, when he returns at the eschaton.

First Corinthians is also the only writing of the Pauline corpus, and in the New Testament overall, where anything is specifically said about a "spiritual body" with which the dead will be resurrected. Judging from the way Paul introduces his discussion of this resurrection body and presents his case for its special character (15.35–49, 52), one may infer that the Corinthians had probably not heard him speak of it before. It is possible that at the time he first taught them about the resurrection of the dead, the apostle himself was not yet familiar with – or had not yet conceived – the idea; but it is equally possible that the notion of a spiritual body emerges only in 1 Corinthians simply because the nature of the resurrection body has only now become an issue. While no such conception appears in 1 Thessalonians 4.13–17, where Paul had already written about the resurrection of the dead, nothing he says there precludes the notion that he advances in 1 Corinthians 15.

Paul had also written nothing to the Thessalonians about a "change" to be experienced by those who will survive until the Lord's return. But again, this was not a matter that was especially pertinent to the situation in the Thessalonian congregation. What makes it pertinent for the argument in 1 Corinthians 15 is the apostle's own statement that "flesh and blood cannot inherit God's reign" (v. 50). If this is so, then everyone will have to "be changed" (*allagēsometha*, v. 51), for the perishable must put on imperishability (vv. 52–54). A similar expectation seems to be reflected in Philippians 3.21 (Christ himself "will transform [*metaschēmatisei*] the body of our humiliation that it may be conformed [*summorphon*] to the body of his glory," NRSV), 2 Corinthians 5.1–5 (v. 4: "we wish not to be unclothed but to be further clothed, so that what is mortal may be swallowed up by life," NRSV), and Romans 8.29 ("those whom he foreknew he also predestined to be conformed [*summorphous*] to the image of his Son," NRSV). The only comparable ideas elsewhere in the New Testament surface in Luke 20.36

(in the resurrection life the children of God will be "like angels") and 1 John 3.2 (what God's children "will be" is not yet disclosed, but they will at least be "like him, for [they] will see him as he is," NRSV; cf. 1 Cor. 13.12; Matt. 5.8).

Ecclesiology

What 1 Corinthians contributes, above all, to a view of the church is the image of the believing community as "one body" with many members (12.12–30). The diversity-within-unity that is portrayed by this image is consistent with the viewpoint reflected in the baptismal statement in Galatians 3.28, which is also echoed in 1 Corinthians 12.13, but the image itself is not present in either Galatians or 1 Thessalonians (the latter certainly earlier than 1 Corinthians, even if the former is not). In the other Paulines the image of the church as a body is found only in Romans and, among those of disputed authenticity, Colossians and Ephesians. Perhaps surprisingly, it appears nowhere else in the New Testament.

Especially in 1 Corinthians, but also in Romans (12.3–8), Paul uses this image in order to emphasize that the diversity (of status, spiritual gifts, and the like) that is represented among those who have been called to belong to Christ does not have to be overcome and must certainly not be exploited. Instead, it is to be affirmed and celebrated as God's way of providing for the needs of the body, and of demonstrating both its unity and that its members are *variously and equally* important for one another (1 Cor. 12.4–11, 12–26). This image of the church is substantially modified in Colossians and Ephesians when Christ is identified as the "head" of the body (Col. 1.18; 2.19; Eph. 1.22–23; 4.15–16; 5.23), a step not taken by Paul in 1 Corinthians, where the head is mentioned as but one of the body's members (12.21).

Because claims about spiritual gifts were a major factor contributing to the disunity that threatened the Corinthian congregation, our letter is also distinctive for the extended comments it provides on the gifts, especially, of prophesying and speaking in tongues. Elsewhere in the undisputed letters, spiritual gifts are mentioned only in 1 Thessalonians 5.19–20 and Romans 12.6–8. In distinction from the lists offered by Paul, those in Ephesians 4.11 and 1 Peter 4.10–11 do not mention such gifts as speaking in tongues, but are restricted to the more practical gifts of ministry.

Finally, 1 Corinthians is also notable for being the only New Testament writing, except for the Synoptic Gospels, in which the words of eucharistic institution are cited (11.23–25). Our letter also provides the earliest (and only New Testament) evidence of how a specific congregation actually observed the eucharist (11.17–22), as well as the earliest reflections, albeit brief, on the importance and meaning of this observance (10.16–17; 11.26; cf. 11.27–34). The version of the words of eucharistic institution transmitted by Paul has special affinities with the version in Luke 22.19–20, in that both include an instruction to "Do this in remembrance" of Jesus (although Paul has it twice and Luke only once), and both refer specifically to the "new" covenant established in Jesus' blood (contrast Matt. 26.26–28 and Mark 14.22–24). That this rite has considerable ecclesiological significance for Paul is evident from his comment that sharing in the Lord's table means celebrating both the new reality of life in (the resurrected-crucified) Christ (10.16) and the oneness of those for whom Christ died (10.17; cf. 8.11–12), and also from his distress at the disorders which have marred its observance in Corinth.

1 CORINTHIANS IN THE CHURCH

The reception of 1 Corinthians by the church began on the day that it was first read to the members of the congregation to whom it was addressed. We have no direct evidence for judging the kind of impact it may have had on them, but there is the indirect evidence of the two or more subsequent Pauline letters to the congregation which have survived as 2 Corinthians, as well as the fact that 1 Corinthians was not suppressed or destroyed by its recipients. However, the first explicit reference to our letter is in *1 Clement*, written in the last decade of the first century, which we may therefore take as the beginning point for some remarks about the theological significance of 1 Corinthians for the church of the early period (through Augustine), in the Reformation era, and today.

The early church

Before considering three examples of theological discussions in the late second through the fifth centuries in which texts and ideas from 1 Corinthians played a prominent role, it is appropriate that we take special note of two earlier writers for whom this letter was particularly important.

One of these is the anonymous author of *1 Clement*, a letter addressed to the church in Corinth by the Christian community in Rome (*c.* 96).[5] Like Paul in 1 Corinthians, he urges the congregation, which is again divided and disordered, to manifest the unity to which it has been called in Christ. In support of his own appeals, he specifically directs the Corinthians to re-read the letter sent to their church by "the blessed Paul, the apostle," in which he had decried their partisan claims about himself, Cephas, and Apollos (*1 Clem.* 47.1–4; cf. 1 Cor. 1.11–13 etc.). Invoking Paul's image of the congregation as one body with many members, he insists with the apostle that even the humblest members of the body are necessary for its proper functioning, and that the stronger have special responsibilities for the weaker (*1 Clem.* 37.5–38.2; 46.5–7). He also follows Paul in praising God's love (*agapē*) as disclosed in Christ, and in declaring that "apart from love nothing is well pleasing to God" (*1 Clem.* 49.1–50.5; cf. 1 Cor. 13). And elsewhere in the letter he draws on 1 Corinthians 15 for arguments to support belief in the resurrection of the dead, representing Christ's resurrection as the first fruits of the coming resurrection, and offering some of his own analogies from nature (*1 Clem.* 24.1–5; cf. 1 Cor. 15.20, 23, 35–41).

The second writer worthy of special notice is Ignatius, the martyred bishop of Antioch (d. 110), who was significantly influenced by Paul's thought, especially as it appears in 1 Corinthians (the Pauline letter most often reflected in the Ignatian correspondence).[6] For example, Ignatius' relatively frequent references to the

---

[5] See, e.g., Donald A. Hagner, *The Use of the Old and New Testaments in Clement of Rome*, NovTSup 34 (Leiden, 1973), 195–209; Andreas Lindemann, *Die Apostolischen Väter I: Die Clemensbriefe I/II*, HNT 17 (Tübingen, 1992); idem, *Paulus im ältesten Christentum. Das Bild des Apostels und die Rezeption der paulinischen Theologie in der frühchristlichen Literatur bis Marcion*, BHT 58 (Tübingen, 1979), 72–82.

[6] See, e.g., Lindemann, *Die Clemensbriefe*, 199–221; Henning Paulsen, *Studien zur Theologie des Ignatius von Antiochien*, Forschungen zur Kirchen- und Dogmengeschichte, 29 (Göttingen,

cross and Jesus' crucifixion (*Eph.* 9.1; 16.2; 18.1; *Trall.* 9.1; 11.2; *Philad.* 8.2; *Smyrn.* 1.1; cf. *Rom.* 5.3; 7.2) clearly owe something to the prominence of Paul's excursus on the meaning of the cross (1 Cor. 1.18–2.16). This is notably the case in *Ephesians* 17–19, where Ignatius describes the cross as an offense (*skandalon*) to unbelievers and the ruler of this age, and contrasts the foolishness of those who are perishing with the knowledge of God that is granted in Christ. Again, in emphasizing the unity of the church, which is a major theme in his letters, Ignatius employs several ecclesiological images that Paul had used in 1 Corinthians. In *Ephesians* 9.1 (cf. *Eph.* 15.3) he refers to believers as stones for God's "temple" (*naos*) who have been prepared for God's "building" (*oikodomē*; cf. 1 Cor. 3.9–17), and elsewhere he is clearly thinking of the church as a body. Although the word "body" (*sōma*) occurs just once in this sense (*Smyrn.* 1.1, "the one body of [Christ's] church"), the image is no less in play when, in two other letters, he refers to believers as "members" (*melē*) of Christ (*Eph.* 4.2; *Trall.* 11.2).[7]

From the latter half of the second century and on into the fifth, passages from 1 Corinthians figured prominently in discussions and controversies, about, especially, Christ's relation to God, the nature of the resurrection and resurrection body, and the relative merits of marriage and virginity. A few remarks about each of these must suffice.

The role of Christ and his relation to God
One of the scriptural passages that came to figure most prominently in discussions about the role of Christ and his relation to God was 1 Corinthians 15.24–28, in which Paul remarks that ultimately Christ will deliver his reign to the Father and himself be subjected to God.[8] At first these statements provoked no special

---

1978); Heinrich Rathke, *Ignatius von Antiochien und die Paulusbriefe*, TU 99 (Berlin, 1967); William R. Schoedel, *Ignatius of Antioch. A Commentary on the Seven Letters of Ignatius*, Hermeneia (Philadelphia, 1985).

[7] However, in *Trall.* 11.2 the image is expanded, as in Colossians and Ephesians, to include the idea of Christ as the "head" of the members.

[8] See, esp., Joseph T. Lienhard, "The Exegesis of 1 Cor 15, 24–28 from Marcellus of Ancyra to Theodoret of Cyrus," *VC* 37 (1983), 340–59; Eckhard Schendel, *Herrschaft und Unterwerfung Christi, 1 Korinther 15, 24–28. Exegese und Theologie der Väter bis zum Ausgang des 4. Jahrhunderts*, BGBE 12 (Tübingen, 1971); Maurice F. Wiles, *The Divine Apostle. The Interpretation of St. Paul's Epistles in the Early Church* (Cambridge, 1967), 73–93.

interest. In both *1 Clement* (50.3) and the (early second century?) letter of *Barnabas* (4.13), as in Colossians and Ephesians, there are matter-of-fact references to the reign of Christ, as if the apostle had said nothing at all about Christ's ever handing the reign over to God. Later, Irenaeus (d. *c.* 200) – who cites 1 Corinthians more than any other Pauline letter – did call attention to both the limited duration of Christ's reign and the Son's own ultimate subjection to God, but there is no indication that he regarded Paul's statements about these as rendering Christ's divinity in any way problematic (*Against Heresies* 5.36.2).[9] The temporary duration of Christ's reigning was also noted by Tertullian (d. *c.* 225), who commented further that this shows the Father and Son are "two separate persons" (*Against Praxeas* 4).[10] Somewhat differently, Origen (d. 254) viewed the text soteriologically, interpreting Christ's subjection as the fulfillment of his saving work, not as the end of his reign (*On First Principles* 3.6.7; *Homilies on Leviticus* 7.2).[11]

This passage became the subject of more focused attention in the fourth century, primarily because of the provocative interpretation of it put forward by Marcellus of Ancyra (d. *c.* 374). Distinguishing the reign of Christ from the reign of God, Marcellus argued that Christ has been appointed to reign only in his humanity and only for the specific purpose of overcoming humanity's fallenness, and that when this purpose is fulfilled his particular reign will come to an end.[12] In opposition to Marcellus, many argued a position akin to Origen's, that Paul meant *Christians* will be subjected to God once the Son's redemptive work has been completed (e.g., Eusebius [d. *c.* 340], *Church Theology* 3.15), others that he meant Christ's human nature would be subjected to God (e.g., Hilary [d. 367], *On the Trinity* 11.40–41), and still others that Paul viewed Christ's subjection as manifesting his concord with God, and thus his divinity (e.g., John Chrysostom [d. 407], *Homilies*

---

[9] Schendel, *Herrschaft und Unterwerfung*, 35–30. For Irenaeus' overall interpretation of Paul, see Rolf Noormann, *Irenäus als Paulusinterpret. Zur Rezeption und Wirkung der paulinischen und deuteropaulinischen Briefe im Werk des Irenäus von Lyon*, WUNT 2/66 (Tübingen, 1994).

[10] Schendel, *Herrschaft und Unterwerfung*, 30–73; Wiles, *The Divine Apostle*, 88–89.

[11] Schendel, *Herrschaft und Unterwerfung*, 81–110; Wiles, *The Divine Apostle*, 89.

[12] Lienhard, "1 Cor 15, 24–28," 342–43; Schendel, *Herrschaft und Unterwerfung*, 111–43; Wiles, *The Divine Apostle*, 89–90.

on 1 Corinthians 39).[13] In this manner, and somewhat ironically, Paul's striking theocentric affirmations in 1 Corinthians, not only in 15.24–28 but also in 3.23 (Christ belongs to God) and 11.3 (God is the head of Christ), eventually came to be drawn into discussions about the nature of the godhead, and to be offered in support of Trinitarian doctrine (e.g., Chrysostom, *Homilies on 1 Corinthians* 26; Ambrosiaster [late 4th century] 239 D; Augustine [354–430], *On the Trinity* 1.8; 6.9).[14]

The nature of the resurrection and resurrection body

From the second century on, discussions about the resurrection of the dead were often focused on the proper interpretation of passages in 1 Corinthians, chapter 15 being, understandably, of prime importance for the subject.[15] Because Paul's statement that "flesh and blood cannot inherit God's reign" (15.50) was regularly used by those of Gnostic outlook to support their unique views of resurrection, that text was frequently at the forefront of the discussion, as both Irenaeus and Tertullian had occasion to point out (Irenaeus, *Against Heresies* 5.9.1; cf. 1.30.13; Tertullian, *On the Resurrection of the Flesh* 48.1).

Christian Gnostics, particularly in the tradition of Valentinus (2nd century), seem to have had a special affinity for Paul's letters, not least for 1 Corinthians.[16] Here, for example, they claimed to

---

[13] These and other references in Wiles, *The Divine Apostle*, 90, nn. 1–4. See also Lienhard, "1 Cor 15, 24–28," 343–53; Schendel, *Herrschaft und Unterwerfung*, 143–200.

[14] There was also concern to demonstrate that the affirmation of "one God, one Lord" (1 Cor. 8.6) was compatible with Trinitarian understandings of the godhead (e.g., Chrysostom, *Homilies on 1 Corinthians* 20; Ambrosiaster 227 B). For the same purpose, Augustine often commented on Paul's description of Christ as "God's wisdom and God's power" (1 Cor. 1.24), which the Manicheans interpreted as a reference to the twofold nature of Christ (e.g., *On the Trinity* 6.1; 7.1–2; cf. 15.3, 6). For the Manichean use of 1 Cor. 1.24, see Augustine's *Against Faustus* 20.2, and the comments by C. P. Bammel, "Pauline Exegesis, Manichaeism and Philosophy in the Early Augustine," *Tradition and Exegesis in Early Christian Writers*, VCS 500 (Aldershot and Brookfield, 1995), XVI, 1–25, here: 5, 6.

[15] A history of the exegesis of some key verses in chapter 15, from the second century through the Council of Chalcedon, is provided by François Altermath, *Du corps psychique au corps spirituel: interpretation de 1 Cor. 15, 35–49*, BGBE 18 (Tübingen, 1977), 52–243.

[16] See, esp., Klaus Koschorke, "Paulus in den Nag-Hammadi Texten. Ein Beitrag zur Geschichte der Paulusrezeption im frühen Christentum," *ZTK* 78 (1981), 177–205. Also, Lindemann, *Paulus im ältesten Christentum*, 97–101, 297–343; Elaine Hiesey Pagels, *The Gnostic Paul. Gnostic Exegesis of the Pauline Letters* (Philadelphia, 1975), esp. 53–94 (1 Corinthians).

find support for their identification of three distinct types of existence (Irenaeus, *Against Heresies* 1.8.3): the "earthly" (*choikoi*, 1 Cor. 15.48), the "natural" (*psychikoi*, 1 Cor. 2.14), and the "spiritual" (*pneumatikoi*, 1 Cor. 2.15).[17] And from here they appropriated Paul's references to a spiritual body (15.44), imperishability, and immortality (15.51–54), as well as his comment about the exclusion of flesh and blood from God's reign (15.50), to authorize their denial of any resurrection of the flesh and their own view of a wholly present, spiritual "resurrection." Such is the view presented, for example, in the late second-century work, *Treatise on the Resurrection* (45.14–46.2; cf. 48.38–49.71), and in *The Gospel of Philip*, from the second century or later, whose author specifically invokes 1 Corinthians 15.50:

Some are afraid lest they rise naked. Because of this they wish to rise in the flesh, and [they] do not know that it is those who wear the [flesh] who are naked. [It is] those who [. . .] to unclothe themselves who are not naked. "Flesh [and blood shall] not inherit the kingdom [of God]." What is this which will not inherit? This which is on us. (56.26–57.8)[18]

Irenaeus offered four principal kinds of argument to refute Gnostic interpretations of this sort.[19] (1) The least developed of these, which may be described as ontological, seems at first to concede a critical point: the flesh to which Paul refers in 1 Corinthians 15.50 is flesh as it is in itself, which indeed is dead and "earthy" (1 Cor. 15.48), and therefore cannot inherit God's reign. But then Irenaeus goes on to argue that this flesh can be saved when it has been enlivened by the Spirit of God, present in Christ (*Against Heresies* 5.9.3). (2) By invoking Pauline texts which contrast living according to the flesh with living according to the Spirit (Rom. 8.8–13; Gal. 5.16–25), he also formulated an ethical argument, claiming that the flesh Paul says is excluded from God's reign is only that which is still bound to carnal desires (ibid., 5.10.2–5.11.2). (3) Irenaeus maintained further, that the language Paul uses, especially in 1 Corinthians 15 where he speaks of that

---

[17] Wiles, *The Divine Apostle*, 29–30.

[18] Translation by Wesley W. Isenberg, in James M. Robinson (ed.), *The Nag Hammadi Library in English* (3rd edn.; San Francisco, 1988), 139–60, here: 144.

[19] Here I am following, in general, Noormann, *Irenäus*, 501–508. Although Wiles, too, identifies four types of argument, he analyses them somewhat differently (*The Divine Apostle*, 43–44).

which "dies," is "raised up," and "lives," cannot apply either to the "soul" or the "spirit" but only to what is mortal, which is the flesh (idem, 5.7.1–2). And finally (4), Irenaeus proposed a christological argument, pointing out that the incarnate Lord himself was flesh and blood, and alleging that redemption could not be by Christ's blood were not blood itself capable of being saved (ibid., 5.14.1–4).

Some variation of the ethical argument (2) was employed by many others who did battle against Gnostic interpretations of 1 Corinthians 15.50, including Tertullian (esp., *On the Resurrection of the Flesh* 50–51; *Against Marcion* 5.10.11; 5.14.4), Clement of Alexandria (*Miscellanies* 2.20; 3.17), Ambrosiaster (270 B), and Augustine (*City of God* 13.22–23; 22.21). It was used as well by Chrysostom (e.g., *Homilies on 1 Corinthians* 42: by "flesh" Paul meant "evil deeds"), who also stressed, however, that while the resurrection body will be of the same substance (*ousia*) as the body that dies, it will be more excellent in quality (ibid., 41).[20] Earlier, the ethical argument had also surfaced in Origen's discussion of the resurrection body (e.g., *On First Principles* 2.10.3), yet his views on this subject were somewhat complex. Although he affirmed the resurrection of bodily matter and stressed the continuity of identity between the body that dies and the one that will be resurrected (ibid.), he also emphasized – quoting copiously from 1 Corinthians 15 – that the resurrection body is not the same as the one that dies (*Against Celsus* 5.18–19). By "the very power and grace of the resurrection," he said, the perishable body will be transformed into an imperishable body of glory, more "refined," "pure," and "advanced" than the mortal body, and therefore truly "spiritual" (*On First Principles* 2.3.2; 2.10.1; 3.6.6).[21]

The superiority of virginity

Finally, Paul's counsels in 1 Corinthians 7 were regularly invoked to support the widely held view that virginity is superior to marriage. Tertullian, for example, gave considerable attention to this chapter (*Exhortation to Chastity*, esp. 3–5; cf. *To His Wife* 1.3; *On Monogamy* 3), above all to the comment that it is better to marry than to burn

---

[20] Wiles, *The Divine Apostle*, 45–46.
[21] See further, ibid., 46–48; Altermath, *Du corps psychique*, 104–24.

(1 Cor. 7.9). He argued that this must be interpreted in the same way as the statement that it is better to lack one eye than two, which obviously does not mean that it is good to lack one eye. Similarly, although Paul says that it is "better" to be married than to be aflame with passion, he is certainly not endorsing marriage as "good" (*Exhortation to Chastity* 3).

At the end of the fourth century Jerome (*c.* 342–420) gave even closer attention to chapter 7 in his essay, *Against Jovinian* (esp. 1.5–13). Jovinian (d. *c.* 405) had held that virginity is not superior to marriage, reasoning in part from the grammar of Paul's question, "Don't you know that your bodies are a temple of the indwelling Holy Spirit?" (1 Cor. 6.19). According to Jovinian, since the apostle uses the singular, "temple," he must mean "that God dwells in all alike," and if this is the case, then believers who are virgins are not superior to those who are married (see *Against Jovinian* 2.19).[22] Jerome's counter arguments also come in substantial part from 1 Corinthians, especially chapter 7. Understandably, he devotes considerable attention to Paul's commendation of singleness, "I wish that all were as I myself am," and also to the apparent qualification of that which follows, "But each has a particular gift from God, one having one kind and another a different kind" (v. 7, NRSV). For Jerome, the inference to be drawn from these statements is not that marriage and virginity are equally good, but that different gifts surely merit different rewards, and that Paul's stated preference marks virginity as the more favored of these two (*Against Jovinian* 1.8).

The Reformation era

In comparison with Galatians and Romans, 1 Corinthians played a relatively insignificant role in the theological discussions of the sixteenth century. The most critical of those involved questions about righteousness, faith, and works, subjects on which this letter

---

[22] David G. Hunter (citing the *Canones in Pauli apostoli epistulas* 33) suggests that Jovinian, in turn, had been arguing against the Priscillianists, who held that the baptized should remain unmarried because Paul says in 1 Cor. 6.19 that they are temples of the Holy Spirit and members of Christ ("Resistance to the Virginal Ideal in Late-Fourth-Century Rome: The Case of Jovinian," *TS* 48 [1987], 45–64, here: 56).

has little to offer, as we have seen – and as a young Philipp Melancthon (1497–1560) readily but also regretfully conceded, noting that rectification (*iustificatione*) is "rather neglected" in this letter.[23] Nonetheless, there were two matters of no small theological importance in the Reformation era for which our letter did serve as an important text of reference.

First, as in the church of the fourth and fifth centuries, chapter 7 was invoked both by those who favored and by those who opposed the view that virginity was especially meritorious. Although the Oxford reformer, John Colet (1466?–1519), was firmly in the tradition of Jerome, arguing from 1 Corinthians 7.1–2 that "marriage has no goodness in it except in so far as it is a necessary remedy for evil,"[24] Melancthon, Martin Luther (1483–1546), and John Calvin (1509–1564) all directly challenged Jerome's interpretation. For example, in his notes to 1 Corinthians 7.1 Melancthon described Jerome as "superstitiously exalting virginity," denied that Paul had specifically commended either marriage or virginity, and concluded that "they are left to any individual's choice in so far only that he chooses one or the other without sin" (*Annotations*, 92/93).

Luther, typically, was more aggressive both in his criticism of Jerome and in his affirmation of marriage. He charged that Jerome not only "misunderstood and misinterpreted Paul" but "wronged himself . . . by not marrying," given that he had admitted to having trouble controlling his strong sexual desires.[25] Moreover, Luther inferred from 1 Corinthians 7 that Paul not only considered marriage as well as virginity to be a gift, but regarded them as equally good in the sight of God. Although he acknowledged the apostle's stated preference for virginity, he attributed that to Paul's opinion

[23] John Patrick Donnelly, S.J. (ed. and trans.), *Annotations on the First Epistle to the Corinthians by Philipp Melancthon*, Reformation Texts With Translation (1350–1650), Biblical Studies, 2 (Milwaukee, 1995), 28/29 (hereafter cited in the text as *Annotations*). This was published by Martin Luther in 1522 without the author's consent, although Melancthon himself published a second exposition of the letter in 1559.

[24] Bernard O'Kelly and Catherine A. L. Jarrott, *John Colet's Commentary on First Corinthians: A New Edition of the Latin Text, with Translation, Annotations, and Introduction*, Medieval and Renaissance Texts and Studies (Binghamton, NY, 1985), 190/191; cf. 196/197 (hereafter cited in the text as *Commentary*).

[25] Martin Luther, *Commentary on 1 Corinthians 7* (1523), in *Luther's Works*, 28 (St. Louis, 1973), 3–56, here: 49, 28 (hereafter cited in the text as *1 Corinthians 7*).

(which Luther shared) that the single have fewer troubles in this life, not to any conviction that virginity is more virtuous and therefore more deserving of a heavenly reward (*1 Corinthians* 7, 47–50). Later, Calvin, too, would remark on Jerome's "false views" about virginity, stressing that Paul regarded it strictly as a gift, and one that was bestowed on only a very few.[26]

Second, Paul's comments about the Lord's supper in 1 Corinthians 10.16–17 and 11.17–34 (esp. vv. 23–26) received close attention in debates about the significance of the mass, which were focused especially on the question of the mode by which Christ was present when it was celebrated. Luther relied heavily on these passages in his broadside on *The Babylonian Captivity of the Church* (1520), in which he argued that the laity no less than the clergy are entitled to receive the eucharistic elements in both kinds, that these elements do not lose their properties as bread and wine when they are transformed into Christ's body and blood, and that the mass is not to be regarded as a sacrifice.[27]

These same passages played an even more important part in controversies that arose among the reformers themselves, especially between Luther and those to his theological left, the most notable of whom was Huldrych Zwingli (1484–1531). Zwingli maintained that Paul's reference to the bread and cup as "participation" in Christ's body and blood (1 Cor. 10.16) has to be interpreted with reference to the apostle's following sentence, where he remarks that "because there is one bread, we who are many are one body, for we all partake of the one bread" (v. 17). According to Zwingli, this means that those who receive the bread and cup do not participate in the literal flesh and blood of Christ, but "unite in one body with the rest of the brethren, which is indeed the body of Christ because that is the body of Christ which believes that the flesh of its author has been slain and his blood

---

[26] John Calvin, *The First Epistle of Paul the Apostle to the Corinthians* (1547), Calvin's Commentaries, 9 (Grand Rapids, 1960), 141–42 (hereafter cited in the text as *First Epistle*); cf. Calvin's *Institutes of the Christian Religion* (1559), The Library of Christian Classics, 21 (Philadelphia, 1960), 2.8.42–43 (hereafter cited in the text as *Institutes*).

[27] In *Luther's Works*, 36 (St. Louis, 1959), 11–126. For Luther's use of the Bible in arguing for his views of the Lord's supper, see Jaroslav Pelikan, *Luther the Expositor: Introduction to the Reformer's Exegetical Writings. Luther's Works*, Companion Volume (St. Louis, 1959), 137–254, esp. 191–236 for the passages in 1 Corinthians.

shed for it."[28] What Christ instituted was thus "a ceremony of commemoration of his having been savagely slain for us," an act of remembering and of faith.[29]

Luther was no less vigorous in rejecting this Zwinglian interpretation of Christ's presence than he was in rejecting the doctrine of transubstantiation, according to which the bread and wine have the properties only of Christ's flesh and blood. Against Rome, Luther argued that the bread and wine retain their ordinary properties, while against Zwingli he maintained that they take on *also* the properties of Christ's actual flesh and blood. He sought to prove this doctrine of "co-presence" (or "consubstantiation") by meeting Zwingli on his own scriptural ground, arguing in large part from 1 Corinthians. According to Luther, "This is my body" (11.24) cannot mean, "This *signifies* my body," and in any case Paul could not have thought of the bread as signifying the church, because he refers to it as *broken* and *distributed* (10.16; 11.24). On this Lutheran reading, therefore, the Pauline texts preclude interpreting the eucharist as participation (*koinōnia*) merely in a subjective "fellowship of faith," and support the view that one participates in the actual body and blood of Christ, which has been given to all in common.[30]

Calvin's understanding of the mode of Christ's presence in the eucharist represents yet a third position, often described as falling somewhere between those of Zwingli and Luther. For our purposes, however, it is enough to observe that Calvin, too, seems to have regarded Paul's comments in 1 Corinthians, especially in chapter 10, as the key to a correct understanding of the traditional but disputed words, "This is my body" (*First Epistle*, 215–17 [on 10.16–17], 242–50 [on 11.23–26]; *Institutes* 4.17–18, esp. 4.17.10, 14–15, 22, 38; 4.18.8).

---

[28] "Letter to Matthew Alber Concerning the Lord's Supper" (1524), *Huldrych Zwingli Writings*. Vol. II: *In Search of True Religion: Reformation, Pastoral and Eucharistic Writings*, Pittsburgh Theological Monograph Series, new series 13 (Allison Park, PA, 1984), 31–44, here: 141.

[29] Ibid., 143. Cf. "Subsidiary Essay on the Eucharist" (1525), idem, II.191–227, esp. 222–23. For an overall presentation of Zwingli's view of the eucharist, see W. P. Stephens, *The Theology of Huldrych Zwingli* (Oxford, 1986), 218–59.

[30] *Confession Concerning Christ's Supper* (1528), *Luther's Works*, 37 (St. Louis, 1961), 161–372 (esp. 303–60); cf. *The Adoration of the Sacrament* (1523), *Luther's Works*, 36, 275–305 (esp. 283–86).

The church today

Because in 1 Corinthians "theology" is so closely bound to pastoral appeals and counsels, this letter appears to have been, historically, somewhat less significant for Christian thought than certain other writings of the Pauline corpus – especially Romans, Galatians, and Ephesians – in which themes of theological importance are more explicitly and fully presented. There is no doubt that specific passages in 1 Corinthians have been employed in the discussion of some disputed issues, as the examples above from the early church and the Reformation era will have shown. But the question remains whether the letter as a whole, read on its own terms, can contribute anything significant to Christian thought today.

Reading Paul's letters on their "own terms" is one of the aims of modern historical-critical inquiry, which is much indebted to the humanism of the Renaissance period as it appears especially in the thought of the sixteenth-century reformers. Already in John Colet's exposition of 1 Corinthians Paul was beginning to emerge as a genuinely historical figure associated with particular times and places, no longer simply the abstract "apostle" whose disembodied voice was heard in Scripture. And when Colet remarks, for example, on Paul's concern for the Corinthians and his strategies for dealing with them (*Commentary*, 74/75, 78/79 [1 Corinthians 1]; 106/107, 108/109 [1 Corinthians 3]), the congregation, too, begins to come into focus, and along with it the real-time context of Paul's thought. This is also the case in Luther, but then most of all and most impressively in Calvin, who sets 1 Corinthians firmly within its historical context by opening his commentary with remarks about the apostle's mission to Corinth, the city itself, and the problems that developed in the congregation he founded there (*First Epistle*, 7–9).

However, as subsequent scholarship has continued to deepen our understanding of the particular circumstances that occasioned 1 Corinthians, at least the *practical* significance of this letter for the church today has become increasingly problematic. For example, there can be no disputing that Paul's counsels to the Corinthians about matters of sex, eating meat from pagan temples, and the employment of spiritual gifts presupposed social conditions and a congregational situation quite specific to his time and to one particular place. It is therefore a serious misappropriation of the letter whenever its counsels are enjoined uncritically on Christians today, who are confronted, both individually and corporately, with social and political realities that are in most cases very different from those in Roman Corinth.

Yet because 1 Corinthians is also, in its own way, a profoundly *theological* letter, it undoubtedly does have a significance for Christian thought that transcends the particularities of its own time and place. The observations offered above about its theological distinctiveness within the New Testament will have already suggested some ways in which this is so. Others can be suggested by reviewing, summarily and by way of conclusion, some of Paul's key theological affirmations in this letter.

(1) Those who have believed and committed themselves to the gospel have been called of God into the company (*koinōnia*) of God's Son, the resurrected-crucified Christ, through whom God has acted for their salvation, and in whom they have been set apart for the service of God.

(2) In belonging to Christ they are in-corporated into one body, established as a believing community of brothers and sisters for whom Christ died. Their initiation into this community has been marked by their baptism and receiving of the Spirit, and accompanied by the bestowal of diverse spiritual gifts, to each individually. The diversity of these gifts does not diminish, but manifests and facilitates the unity with which they have been graced.

(3) Believers have been called to serve God, both individually and corporately, in an age that is swiftly passing away. Moreover, although this present age can offer humanity no real life or hope because it is ruled by forces that are hostile to the purposes of God, it nonetheless continues to tyrannize humanity with its claims, as if these could be ultimate and life defining.

(4) In Christ, believers have been delivered from these de-humanizing and death-dealing claims, and summoned to live in the world "as not" in the world. This summons is not predicated on the irrelevance of the present age, but on their belonging to

Christ, and through Christ to God. The gospel therefore neither requires them to withdraw from the world nor allows them to be indifferent to it, but affirms it as the setting in which they have been called to serve God.

(5) The life of the believing community and the lives of its individual members, as they seek to be obedient to God's call in particular times and places, are defined and graced with purpose by God's love as disclosed in the cross. This love is at once God's power for salvation and the criterion by which all faithful service of God is measured.

(6) God's love also nurtures and warrants the community's hope, which is to bear the image of Christ, to participate in God's reign where he is "all in all," and to know God even as one has already and always been known by God, because all things will have been wholly and without reservation subjected to God's love.

Select bibliography

COMMENTARIES

Barrett, Charles Kingsley. *The First Epistle to the Corinthians*, BNTC (London, 1968).
A deservedly influential commentary by a leading interpreter of Paul's letters and thought.

Conzelmann, Hans. *1 Corinthians. A Commentary on the First Epistle to the Corinthians*, Hermeneia (Philadelphia, 1975).
Translated from the first German edition of 1969, which appeared in the important Kritisch-exegetischer Kommentar über das Neue Testament. Especially valuable for identifying key issues, although the author's own conclusions are often stated quite summarily.

Fee, Gordon D. *The First Epistle to the Corinthians*, NICNT (Grand Rapids, 1987).
An important commentary, by far the most thorough and detailed of those recently published in English on this letter.

Hays, Richard B. *First Corinthians*, Interpretation (Louisville, 1997).
A well-informed, highly readable commentary, especially valuable for engaging the key theological issues.

Horsley, Richard A. *1 Corinthians*, ANTC (Nashville, 1998).
Emphasizes Roman imperial society as the context of the letter, and that Paul was intent on developing his Corinthian assembly as an exclusive, alternative community set over against the world.

Robertson, Archibald T., and Alfred Plummer. *A Critical and Exegetical Commentary on the First Epistle of St Paul to the Corinthians*, ICC (2nd edn.; Edinburgh, 1914).
A classic among English commentaries, still worth consulting for certain philological details.

Schrage, Wolfgang. *Der erste Brief an die Korinther*, EKKNT 7 (3 vols.; Zürich/Braunschweig/Neukirchen-Vluyn, 1991–).
Without peer among the commentaries on 1 Corinthians. No other is so

comprehensive and well informed, exhibits such balanced judgment on disputed issues, or deals so insightfully with the letter's theology.

Weiss, Johannes. *Der erste Korintherbrief*, KEK (9th edn.; Göttingen, 1910). The predecessor volume to Conzelmann's (see above) in the KEK series, this remains a classic among German commentaries.

Wolff, Christian. *Der erste Brief des Paulus an die Korinther*, THKNT 7 (Berlin, 1996).
In accord with the aims of the series in which it is published, particularly attentive to the theological aspects of the letter.

STUDIES

The following have been selected from among the book-length studies available in English which have been cited in the footnotes. All of them either deal specifically with the theology of 1 Corinthians or contribute in some way to an understanding of the letter's theology. It should be noted, however, that many of the most important theological studies of 1 Corinthians have appeared as essays on particular passages or topics. A number of these, along with additional monographs, may be found in the footnotes, where they are often grouped together in the notes linked to paragraphs in which the discussion of a passage or topic is introduced.

Barth, Karl. *The Resurrection of the Dead* (London, 1933).

Beker, J. Christiaan. *Paul the Apostle: The Triumph of God in Life and Thought* (Philadelphia, 1980).

Brown, Alexandra R. *The Cross and Human Transformation. Paul's Apocalyptic Word in 1 Corinthians* (Minneapolis, 1995).

Chow, John K. *Patronage and Power: A Study of Social Networks in Corinth*, JSNTSup 75 (Sheffield, 1992).

Clarke, Andrew D. *Secular and Christian Leadership in Corinth: A Socio-Historical and Exegetical Study of 1 Corinthians 1–6*, AGJU 18 (Tübingen, 1993).

De Boer, Martinus C. *The Defeat of Death. Apocalyptic Eschatology in 1 Corinthians 15 and Romans 5*, JSNTSup 22 (Sheffield, 1988).

Dunn, James D. G. *The Theology of Paul the Apostle* (Grand Rapids, 1998).

Gooch, Peter D. *Dangerous Food. 1 Corinthians 8–10 in Its Context*. Studies in Christianity and Judaism, 5 (Waterloo, Ontario, 1993).

Hay, David M. (ed.). *Pauline Theology*, II: *1 and 2 Corinthians* (Minneapolis, 1993).

Hurd, John Coolidge, Jr. *The Origin of I Corinthians* (London, 1965).

Martin, Dale B. *The Corinthian Body* (New Haven, CT, 1995).

Martin, Ralph P. *The Spirit and the Congregation. Studies in I Corinthians 12–15* (Grand Rapids, 1984).

Meeks, Wayne A. *The First Urban Christians: The Social World of the Apostle Paul* (New Haven, CT, 1983).

Mitchell, Margaret M. *Paul and the Rhetoric of Reconciliation. An Exegetical Investigation of the Language and Composition of 1 Corinthians*, HUT 28 (Tübingen, 1992; repr. Louisville, KY, 1993).

Murphy-O'Connor, Jerome. *St. Paul's Corinth: Texts and Archaeology*, GNS 6 (Collegeville, MN, [1990? © 1983]).

Rosner, Brian S. *Paul's Scripture and Ethics: A Study of 1 Corinthians 5–7*, AGJU 22 (Leiden, 1994).

Theissen, Gerd. *The Social Setting of Pauline Christianity: Essays on Corinth* (Philadelphia, 1982).

Willis, Wendell Lee. *Idol Meat in Corinth: The Pauline Argument in 1 Corinthians 8 and 10*, SBLDS 68 (Chico, CA, 1985).

Index of references

Index of names

Index of subjects